How to Make a Budget Work For You

Heather Schisler

© Copyright 2017 Mile51 Media, LLC
All rights reserved. This book or any portion thereof may not be reproduced or used in any manner whatsoever without the express written permission of the publisher except for the use of brief quotations in a book review.
Printed in the United States of America
First Printing, 2017

Printable Documents		iii
Your 31-Day Budget Plan		vii
Day 1	Set Big Financial Goals	1
Day 2	Why You Need to Make a Budget	7
Day 3	How to Evaluate Your Assets	10
Day 4	Summarize Your Debts	14
Day 5	Review Your Spending Habits	19
Day 6	List Everything You Buy Each Week	25
Day 7	Create a Monthly Expense Chart	29
Day 8	Plan for Yearly Expenses	32
Day 9	Plan for Personal Fun Money	37
Day 10	Dividing Your Expenses into Categories	43
Day 11	Prioritize Your Budget Categories	47
Day 12	Make a List of All Your Income	53
Day 13	Combine Your Income and Expenses	59
Day 14	Assigning Amounts to Each Category	65
Day 15	Handling Additional Categories	70
Day 16	How to Handle Additional Income	75

Day 17	Determine Cash & Set-Back Categories	79
Day 18	Managing Your Budget on a Daily Basis	85
Day 19	Tracking Your Expenses Daily	91
Day 20	Communicate Consistently	95
Day 21	Balance Your Income Before Spending	101
Day 22	Track & Carry Over Set-Back Accounts	105
Day 23	Review & Maintain Your Budget Frequently	109
Day 24	Create a Debt Reduction Plan	113
Day 25	Plan for Unexpected Expenses	117
Day 26	Plan for the Future	121
Day 27	Don't Forget to Give	125
Day 28	Track Progress Towards Your Goals Monthly	129
Day 29	Share Your Successes With Others	133
Day 30	Encourage Others	137
Day 31	Teach Your Children	141

Printable Documents

There are ten important budgeting documents that you will need to complete the activities in this book. You can download these printable documents directly from my website. All you need to do is go to the following website and enter your name and email address along with where you purchased the book, and I'll send you the documents for you to download.

http://www.passionforsavings.com/budget-worksheets

Here are the ten documents you will use as you work through this book:

> Financial Goals Worksheet
> Assets Inventory Worksheet
> Debt Summary Worksheet
> Weekly Expense Chart
> Monthly Expense Chart
> Infrequent Expense Chart
> Category Summary Worksheet
> Income Planning Worksheet
> Budget Planning Worksheet
> Budget Spreadsheet

How to Make a Budget Work for You

All of these are updated and available for you to download and print. Just visit the website to get your free copy!

Your 31-Day Budget Plan

Day 1- Set financial goals.
Take a deep breath and just take a moment to dream... sometimes we can't see past our own two feet when it comes to budgeting. This chapter helps you walk through setting financial goals and starting down the path towards creating a budget.

Day 2 - Why do you need to make a budget?
One of the most important aspects of budgeting is the "why." Everyone needs to know exactly why they are creating a budget and exactly what you hope to accomplish with your budget. These goals will guide other important decisions in your family's budget. Don't skip this step!

Day 3 - Evaluate your assets.
This is the first step in creating your own personal household budget. You want to start by taking inventory of everything your family owns and evaluating your assets. I realize it's easy to say, "I don't have anything," but this chapter will give you some examples and worksheets to help you complete this task.

Day 4 - Summarize your debts.
Once you've listed your personal assets, it's also important to detail your current debts. This chapter goes over the **Debt Summary Worksheet** and explains

How to Make a Budget Work for You

how to list out your debts and how your debt applies to your personal budget.

Day 5 - Review your spending habits.
They say every family has a "Spender" and a "Saver." Read the list of four Spending Personalities and determine which personality best describes you. This is a great way to start identifying your money habits.

Day 6 - List everything you buy each week
You knew this one was coming, didn't you? You can't create a budget until you know what you are spending. Taking time to evaluate what you are currently spending will help you identify areas of excess and also help you plan your budget to accommodate your family's personal needs in each area.

Day 7 - Create a **Monthly Expense Chart**
Once you have listed out your weekly expenses it's a good idea to also list monthly expenses you have. This includes things like your mortgage, car payment, insurance and other larger expenses you pay on a monthly basis.

Day 8 - Plan for yearly expenses.
The final step in evaluating your spending habits is to list out yearly, quarterly, or semiannual expenses. Things like Christmas gifts, life insurance, vacations, etc., all fall in this infrequent yearly category. These are important items to plan for so that when the expense rolls around each year, you will already have the money set aside in your budget.

Your 31-Day Budget Plan

Day 9 - Plan for personal fun money.
If I had a marriage-saving tip, as far as being on the same page with your budget, this is it! Personal fun money, no matter how big or small, will help you have a little bit of freedom within your budget and help you avoid the devastating spending sprees.

Day 10 - Divide your expenses into categories.
Are you ready to start creating your budget? This chapter highlights the different ways to group your expenses to start creating budget categories. Once you have a list of expenses, creating categories should be relatively easy.

Day 11 - Prioritize your budget categories.
This is the hard part of creating your budget-- determining which categories are most important. If you have a flexible income (meaning you make a different amount each month), then this step is very important. You will want to make sure you take some time to think through which items are the most important to your family.

Day 12 - Make a list of all your income.
It doesn't matter how much you make or how many different income streams you have, knowing exactly what you expect to bring in during the year will help you effectively budget your income into your category structure.

Day 13 - Combine your income & expenses.
Combining your list of budget categories with your income is where you get into the fine details of creating your budget.

How to Make a Budget Work for You

Day 14 - Assign amounts to each category.
Each category on your list has to have a budget amount. This could be $0 all the way up to your expected need for this category. Remember, your budget can't be greater than your income, so you may have to make sacrifices at this point to stay on budget and avoid going into debt each month.

Day 15 - How to handle additional categories
What do you do when you have more categories of spending than you have income? This day walks you through determining what to do with those extra categories and how to handle flexible income.

Day 16 - How to handle additional income
If you have additional income or unexpected income that shows up during the year, it is important to have a plan for that extra income. This post explains several options for handling unexpected or additional income streams.

Day 17 - Determine cash & set-back categories.
There are two different types of budget categories. You will need to take the time during this day to work through each category in your budget and determine if it is a Cash or Set-Back category.

Day 18 - Manage your budget on a daily basis.
Once you have your budget set up and you're ready to roll, there are a few tips and tricks for helping you manage your budget on a daily basis. This post highlights how to keep up with your budget and maintain it for everyday use. The more you utilize a

Your 31-Day Budget Plan

budget, the easier the daily aspects of budgeting become.

Day 19 - Tracking your expenses daily.
Everyone has a different method of tracking expenses. This post highlights several of my favorite methods for tracking expenses. There isn't a right or wrong method, so take some time to read over the options and choose the method that works best for you.

Day 20 - Communicate consistently.
A budget doesn't work if everyone involved isn't communicating and on the same page. This one tip will help you stick to your budget for the long term; it is so important to make sure you are communicating openly and honestly in order to have a successful budget!

Day 21 - Balance your income before spending.
If you are living paycheck to paycheck, or you have very little wiggle room in your budget, make sure you read this post on balancing your income. It is so important to make sure that your budget is meeting your own personal needs, and this post outlines one of the best ways to keep your budget on track and keep yourself from overspending and running out of money.

Day 22 - Track & carry over set-back accounts.
One of the first arguments my husband and I had over money had to do with this topic. When you have categories that have excess in them, this post outlines how to handle that money based on the category purpose.

Day 23 - Review & maintain your budget frequently.

How to Make a Budget Work for You

Having a budget is a little bit like having another child-- you have to make sure you are spending ample time managing and maintaining your budget so that it is accurate and effective. A budget that isn't maintained will quickly fall apart.

Day 24 - Create a debt reduction plan.
One of my favorite aspects of budgeting is that you can begin to pay down debt. This post walks you through the method for identifying and beginning to attack debt.

Day 25 - Plan for unexpected expenses.
We have all had those emergencies come up in our life that we weren't planning for. Having a budget allows you to plan not only for the expected but also for unexpected expenses.

Day 26 - Plan for the future.
Saving for retirement and the future is an important aspect of a sound financial plan. It's important to try to not only plan for today but to save for the future, as well. If you are spending all of your income, then this may be difficult, or you may need to tackle debt first. But regardless, this is something that should be in your budget sooner rather than later.

Day 27 - Don't forget to give.
My *favorite* thing to do with money is to give it away. I love giving--over the years I have found that it's such a blessing, and having a solid budget in place allows our family to give when needs around us arise.

Your 31-Day Budget Plan

Day 28 - Track progress towards your goals monthly.
Each month, take the time to track the progress towards your goals. Seeing long-term goals in light of current successes always helps to put your plan in perspective and motivates you to continue on a solid path.

Day 29 - Share your successes with others.
As you begin to win with money, make sure you are sharing your budgeting process and financial successes with others. Not only will you be an encouragement to others, but you will also motivate yourself as you look back over all you have accomplished.

Day 30 - Encourage others.
Encourage others to join you in creating a budget. So many people know they need to get control of their finances, but they don't know how to make a budget, and your encouragement can help others start down the path towards a balanced approach to budgeting.

Day 31 - Teach your children.
Some things are better caught than taught, but budgeting is something that you can do both ways. Leading by example is the best way to teach our kids financial responsibility, but you can also check out this chapter for ways you can get your kids involved in the entire process.

Day 1

Set Big Financial Goals

Documents You Will Need:

> **Financial Goals Worksheet**

One of the things that I am passionate about is budgeting. I was blessed to have parents who always taught me from a young age to budget my money; however, it wasn't until I was married with kids that I learned the value of a daily, monthly, and yearly budget!

Each week, I receive emails from so many people who are trying to figure out how to save money, and I really believe the only way to start is by getting control of your budget. You could grab a lot of deals, "save a lot of money," and still be spending more and more. Creating and living within a budget is the first step to financial freedom, which in the end is my goal for each and every one of you, so we are going to spend a lot of time talking about the steps you can take (both small and large) to create a better budget for you and your family.

How to Make a Budget Work for You

The Importance of Setting Goals

I think it is so important, regardless of what you are trying to accomplish, that you keep your goals in mind. I can promise you that there will be times that working within the bounds of a budget won't seem easy, and during those tough times it's the larger picture, the end goal, that keeps you going, so I want you to start off your budget journey by setting three goals. These should be larger goals because we will break the smaller short-term goals out of these later on.

Everyone will have a different set of goals. Yours may be to pay off college loans. Or you may need to stop spending more than you make to stop the debt cycle. Others may be wanting to pay cash for a family vacation. Your goal is completely unique to you and your situation. Remember: these are your dreams and your goals, so set your hopes high. You will be amazed in hindsight at what you are able to accomplish when you focus and set your mind on a path towards a goal.

Goal-setting as much about setting a plan in place as it is dreaming. It's hard to accomplish something if you don't know where you are going. One of my favorite quotes is, "Begin with the end in mind." That's exactly what I want you to do--set a goal that you can work towards. Having a goal or an "end" helps you see and track your progress. Your goals are your filter through which you make decisions on a daily basis. When we were saving to pay off our mortgage, I remember saying over and over again, "I can't buy that because we want to pay off our house." It was my filter for big and small decisions.

Set Big Financial Goals

If you are searching for the right goals for your family, I wanted to share a few ideas with you. In the past some, of our financial goals have consisted of paying down debt, paying off our house, and paying cash for a car, cash-flowing the birth of our children, saving for college, saving more for retirement, and giving more. Three of our past and current goals include saving to pay cash for a house, saving for a new car so that we can replace one of ours, and saving for a summer vacation. All three of these things keep us moving forward in the weekly ins and outs of budgeting, which happens on a daily basis.

So let's get practical. Each day I want to give you a take-away, a little homework to keep you on track :)

Day 1: Write Down 3 Financial Goals

Take some time right now to jot down three financial goals for you and your family. You can use the **Financial Goals Worksheet** to help you walk through the process. Put the goals list somewhere you can see it: in front of your computer work area, on your refrigerator, in your purse—wherever you will see it when you need a little encouragement.

Budgeting with Kids:

If you have kids, make sure you take the time to talk over these goals with them now. You may not have ever talked about money before, but it is important because you will need their help over the next few months as you work your budget. They may have to realize that there are times they can't have everything they want,

How to Make a Budget Work for You

and keeping those budgets and goals in mind as a family can help everyone to learn the value of money.

Day 2

Why You Need to Make a Budget

Yesterday, we talked about how to set financial goals, which I really believe is a critical step to achieving a great budget, and today I want to talk about the second piece to that puzzle: the why. I don't know if I have ever talked to a person who says it's a bad idea to have a budget. Almost everyone I meet thinks it's a good idea, but so many people forget to personalize the "why" in a budget... Why do YOU want a budget? What is a budget going to help you accomplish?

The Importance of Why

This might be one area where each and every one of us will have a different answer. It is important not only to set big goals but to know why you're trying to make a budget, as well. Do you need a budget? Is it just something you've always wanted? Maybe it's something you believe can change your life!

To be honest, the "why" in my budget changes just about every year. Just like I like to sit down and evaluate my financial goals with my husband each year, I also think it's important to know why you're trying to live within a budget. For me, I'm a spender. If I don't

How to Make a Budget Work for You

have a budget, I have a HUGE tendency to overspend. So having a budget provides the boundaries I need to keep spending under control. It gives me guidelines that I can work within and allows me to make purchases without feeling guilty later on (as long as the expenses are provided for in the budget).

A budget is also a means of communication between me and my husband. It allows us to set goals together and to decide what our priorities are; it also allows us both freedom within the bounds of the budget to make purchasing decisions. There's little to no fighting or arguing that happens at our house over money because the decisions about what we are going to buy are made ahead of time. We are choosing where to spend our money together, and that gives us great unity in our marriage and in our family.

Lastly, I think a budget is important because it allows you to plan for upcoming expenses. I'm a firm believer that you shouldn't go into debt, but that requires planning, so a budget allows me to plan for expected expenses as well as unexpected ones. Without a budget, I wouldn't be able to accomplish my financial goals, so that's another important reason why I believe in budgeting.

So, let's get practical. Each day, I want to give you a take-away, a little homework to keep you on track :)

Day 2: Come Up With 3 Reasons "Why"
Take some time right now to jot down three reasons you need a budget. Then, the real challenge is to share

these reasons with at least two people you know. Your husband could be one; a friend could be one; or a relative, family member, or even a neighbor. The conversation might look something like this:

"You know, I've been thinking I need to get serious about sticking to a budget because...."

You fill in the blank. Remember, everyone's reasons are different, depending on your financial situation and where you are in your money saving journey. It's important to share these reasons because it will help you internalize your resolve to both create and, more importantly, stick to your budget.

Budgeting with Kids:

If you have kids, make sure you take the time to talk about the reasons why you are starting to create a budget. Especially if you haven't ever had a budget before, your kids will quickly notice the limits on spending, and they will more than likely ask questions, so involving them early on in the process allows them to take ownership of what you are doing and why. If you have older kids, you may find they are jumping on the bandwagon and more willing to help reduce expenses because they understand the benefits involved in making a budget and sticking to it.

Day 3

How to Evaluate Your Assets

Documents You Will Need:

> **Assets Inventory Worksheet**

Now that we have covered setting goals and determining why we want to create a budget, we are going to start diving into the details of putting together your personal plan. One of the first things you need to do when creating a budget is evaluate where you stand. That includes what you own, what you earn, and what you owe. All three of these are critical in balancing your family's budget and determining what your priorities are.

How to Evaluate Your Assets

First, let's start with the basics of assets. Simply put, assets are things you own. When it comes to your family and household, I'm talking about anything with significant value such as a house, a car, a boat, four-wheeler, motorcycles, and other high-value items your family might own. What is important is to determine where the money we have had in the past has gone. I really believe that if you're going to get a budget to work, you have to be open, honest, and realistic with

How to Evaluate Your Assets

yourself. So take a look around your house for anything of value and start making a list.

I am going to jump out on a limb here and say that most of you instantly think, "Well I don't have anything valuable," but you might want to stop and rethink that one. Let me phrase this another way to help get the ideas rolling. Do you have anything in your home you could sell for money? If you could sell it to someone else for, let's say, more than $100, add it to your list of assets. So now we are talking about things like computers, TVs, iPads, iPods, Kindles, etc. These are assets that have value and items that could also be sold if you needed the money for an emergency fund or to pay off debt, so those go on the list, as well.

As you make your list of assets in your home, remember to think about non-tangible assets: things you may own but you aren't going to see or touch or feel on a daily basis. This might include things like your retirement 401k, your college savings fund, your bank accounts, and savings bonds you got when you were a kid. These should all go on the list, as well. Now, hopefully, your ideas are flowing and you're starting to get a good idea of the assets around your house. I promise I'm not going to tell you to sell everything. My goal is simply for you to think about what you have and where you have been spending your money. Also, consider the importance of each of these items and how frequently you use them. There is a tendency when you aren't budgeting to buy items you want without calculating if you really need or can afford an item. That's the mindset we want to stop. In order for a budget to work for you, you need to take an active, intentional approach to your money, and this is the first step!

How to Make a Budget Work for You

So, let's get practical. Each day, I want to give you a take-away, a little homework to keep you on track :)

Day 3: Create an Assets Inventory

Print out the **Assets Inventory Worksheet** and start listing items you own that have value. You may need to print the page several times to cover all your assets.

1. List your large and small assets as well as assets that are both tangible and non-tangible.

2. Note how important the asset is to you by numbering each asset with a number between 1 and 5, with 1 being an item you don't use very often and a 5 being something that is very important to you and your family.

3. Lastly, I want you to estimate the value of the asset. You don't have to be exact, but try to estimate the value based on what you could sell the item for, not the price you paid. For example, a TV you purchased five years ago for $600 is likely not worth $600 still, because the same TV new would probably only cost a few hundred dollars now, so a used TV has even less value. Next to the value of the item, draw an arrow pointing either up or down. This indicates the direction the value of this item is moving. Something you might notice is that most of the "assets" you own are going down in value. This is an important realization for the future of your budget, so don't skip this last step!

How to Evaluate Your Assets

Budgeting with Kids:

Getting your kids involved with creating your Assets Inventory is a great way to help your kids become grateful for what they have. Try creating this list one night at the dinner table. You might not get it finished completely, but you could have a great conversation about the things you own and their values as well as which items go up in value versus which items go down in value. These conversations are so critical in shaping the opinions of our kids about money.

Little kids can get involved in making a list of everything your family owns. Even if they don't understand valuation and assets, this is a great time to talk about being grateful for the things that we have been blessed with and how important it is to take care of the things that we have been given.

Day 4

Summarize Your Debts

Documents You Will Need:

> **Debt Summary Worksheet**

I hope you took time to complete the **Assets Inventory** from Day 3. Today we're going to talk about something that's not quite as fun as what we own. It's time to get serious about what you owe. Not just the monthly household bills, but the long-term outstanding debts that can eat up your weekly budget quickly if you're not careful to get these under control.

How to Summarize Your Debts

First, let's start with the basics of debts. Simply put, debts are things you owe. Some of the most common debts include your household mortgage, car loans, student loans, boat loans, and credit card debt. All of these items require you to repay the amount you borrowed plus interest. When we are talking about debt, make sure you are looking at all of your debts combined. It's easy to only focus on credit card debt and to forget that those house mortgages and car loans are also forms of debt.

Summarize Your Debts

This process isn't completely focused on paying down debt, but I am a firm believer in being debt-free, and one of my long-term goals for you in having a budget that works is that you're able to start paying money towards reducing your debts. Nothing makes a budget function better than eliminating those monthly expenses on items you bought in the past! Every dollar you pay towards interest is money that could be spent on this month's budget, so in the long term, reducing debt actually frees up your budget to work more efficiently.

When you are making a list of your debts, be sure to include both current and past debts that may still be outstanding. A lot of times, these out-of-date debts can be settled for a fraction of the balance, so you will want to make sure you're getting the best overall picture of what you owe. As we list the debts, let's list the person owed and the outstanding balance along with the monthly payment. That will help you later on when you start building your budget.

So, let's get practical. Each day, I want to give you a take-away, a little homework to keep you on track :)

Day 4: Summarize Your Debts

Print out the **Debt Summary Worksheet** and start listing items you owe money on. You may need to print the page several times to cover all your debts.

> 1. **List your debts from smallest to largest.** Remember to list the person/company owed.

How to Make a Budget Work for You

2. List the outstanding balance.

3. List the monthly minimum payment (You'll need this amount later for your **Budget Planning Worksheet**).

Budgeting with Kids:

Something that kids really don't understand is debts, because most kids live on cash only. They get their allowance and they spend it. I know my five-year-old often asks if I can "loan" him the money to buy a toy that he's saving for before he has enough. Those last few weeks of waiting (and working) teach a valuable lesson to kids that we don't spend money we don't have. If you have little ones who you often give advances in allowance to, or loan them money to buy a toy they want when they haven't worked and saved for it, this is a valuable time to teach kids about budgeting, saving, and not going into debt.

While it's a hard lesson to learn, it's important for kids to learn to spend within their means and not to go into debt over toys, candy, food, movies, and more. This will also help to teach them the value of planning and preparing by having a budget!

Day 5

Review Your Spending Habits

In every relationship, there is a spender and a saver. Personally, I'm a spender, which is why I'm in love with my budget! I completely understand that to most people that sounds backwards. You would think someone who loves to spend money would be anti-budget, but for me a budget allows me the ability to spend without guilt as long as I'm within the budget! Budgeting has also forced me to look at my spending habits and make adjustments. I began using coupons so that I wouldn't have to reduce my clothing budget after we had kids, so in a way, spending and budgeting can work together.

How to Analyze Your Spending Habits

I love to talk about spending habits because it's so personal to me. I tend to be a spender, and my husband is a saver. I remember when we first got married my husband used to joke that he loved to save as much as I loved to spend. There are a few different types of spenders and savers that I want to go over. My hope is that you can identify with one of these different spending or saving habits.

The Daily Spender - Some spenders like to spend money continuously. This doesn't have to be large amounts each day but may be smaller, consistent amounts. These are the people who eat out every day, go to Starbucks on the way home, shop weekly at the mall, and have other small habitual expenditures that add up. The problem with the daily spender is that they can spend money mindlessly. While they may not ever feel like they are making big purchases, these spenders will overspend by purchasing large amounts of small-value items.

The Big Spender – These spenders tend to purchase larger luxury items. Well, sometimes they are *small* high-priced luxury items. These are probably the people you think of as spenders. They enjoy quality, and they enjoy shopping for just the right item. Sometimes the big spender appears flashier than the daily spender, which is why they are more of the stereotype. Being a big spender isn't necessarily bad as long as you are planning for your purchases and you are able to afford them. The problem is when your spending goes beyond your budget or causes you to suffer in other, more necessary, areas such as savings.

The Saver - The saver typically is very strict with their money. They don't make purchases easily because they really enjoy saving money and seeing the numbers in the bank account go up. I often find that savers don't like budgets because they don't want to admit the realistic expenses of everyday life. Savers like to hold on to their money more than they like to spend it, so they look for ways to avoid buying things they don't need. Purchases are driven by necessity more than desire. While saving money is great, you also want to make sure you are providing for your needs and planning for expenses rather than just pulling the money out of savings when you need it. The downfall to being a saver is typically failure to plan for non-monthly expenses or emergencies. If you're a saver, make sure you're being

Review Your Spending Habits

realistic in your budget while still saving as much as you can.

The Splurger – Sometimes the splurger appears to be what is affectionately referred to as a "tightwad." You know the person who never spends money, never spends money, never spends money, then goes and buys a TV. The splurger often is running their budget off emotions. They save and save and save, or don't spend because they feel they don't have the money to afford anything, until they finally splurge and spend on something big that may be out of the budget. If you think you're a splurge, it's important to set up a budget that provides for your needs so you don't end up overspending on items that you haven't planned to buy.

Day 5: Review Your Spending Habits

Look over the four different types of spenders above. Which one are you? What are the downfalls to how you spend? To be honest, I'm not sure than any one spending habit is better or worse than the others. They all have their own negatives, and the value in reviewing your spending habits isn't trying to change your habits but to more effectively manage your spending habits within your budget. Here are four ways you can manage your spending habits within your budget:

The Daily Spender - Manage daily spending by setting up more detailed budget categories. You may want to have a weekly budget category for Starbucks that only has $5 per week rather than the $30 you may currently be spending. This gives you the freedom to still go to Starbucks, but within reason and within your budget.

How to Make a Budget Work for You

The Big Spender - If you like to purchase big ticket items, you will want to set back money for these big-purchase items--maybe a Wish List budget that gets $10 to $20 a paycheck towards your current Wish List item. When the money is in the budget, you can then purchase the item you want.

The Saver - If you are a saver, make sure you go over your budget in detail and make sure your expenses are realistic. You may be able to get by on $40 a week for gas some weeks, but long-term, is that a realistic amount? Don't sell your budget categories short because overspending will cost you more than planning correctly.

The Splurger - If you tend to deprive yourself then splurge, it's important to plan more effectively. You want to base your budget off monthly or annual numbers, not what you think you spend weekly. This will help you better evaluate what you spend long-term so that you aren't dipping into savings or an emergency fund on a frequent basis.

Budgeting with Kids:

Even kids have a spending habit style. These can be trained and molded by parents' spending habits, so don't forget to evaluate the influence your spending habits may have on your kids. I know that, personally, both my husband and I have been influenced by the way our parents viewed money, so this is something you want to be aware of when you talk with your kids about money.

Review Your Spending Habits

While bringing out our kids' strengths in money is important, it's also important for us to help them balance their own spending habits at an early age. For example, if you have a Spender for a kid, help them set up envelopes or separate piggy banks for spending, saving, and giving. If you have a Saver, encourage them to buy a gift for someone else so they can still learn to make wise financial decisions. Maybe you can help them give some away or buy a gift during the holidays, something that helps them plan and make wise choices that they might not typically make on their own.

With my kids, my Spender is a giver, so he constantly wants to give all his money away. I have to encourage him to give a portion and also to save some at the same time. One of my other kids isn't a spender. She rarely buys anything and, honestly, she doesn't keep up with her money well, so I am working with her on staying organized and planning for purchases so that she learns to take better care of her money- because I know that's a skill she will need later in life.

Day 6

List Everything You Buy Each Week

Documents You Will Need:

> **Weekly Expense Chart**

Are you ready to get started in the details of creating your budget? I hope you joined me the first few days and didn't skip the activities because they have laid a very important foundation for the next few steps in our budget. Today, we are going to talk about listing out everything you buy in a week. This is the first step in determining what categories need to be included in your overall budget.

How to Determine What You Buy In a Week

At first glance, this is going to sound really, really easy. But after the first five to ten items, this list will become more complex. I promise you that the more detailed your list of items you buy, the better your budget will be in the end. The idea here is that if you don't know where you are spending money, then it will be hard to know what categories to create. One of the things I hear from friends all the time is that they don't know where to start when they make a budget, and that's largely because they don't know how much money they are spending currently or what they buy on a frequent basis. Without that knowledge, you can get lost trying to sit down and create a list of "categories" and, most

How to Make a Budget Work for You

likely, in the end your budget won't be realistic enough to last longer than a few months.

Here are a few things you want to remember:

Don't forget the basics – Start by thinking through each day of your week. Do you normally eat out as a family on Tuesday night before baseball practice? Or do you go shopping on Monday mornings? Try to remember things like gas for your car and lunch money for the kids (or yourself). This is a list of items you're currently buying. Don't try to cut things out, yet. That will come later. You want to make sure you're being realistic about what you're spending your money on, so don't try to pretend you don't buy anything each week :) If you need a little help, try pulling out the receipts from your wallet. That will give you a good idea of what you purchase on a daily basis.

Non-cash expenses – If you have weekly expenses that deduct from your bank account, make sure those are included, too. If you are paid on a weekly basis, then you may have more auto-deducts on a weekly basis than others. That's ok. The important thing is to list these expenses.

Kids and allowance – If you pay your kids an allowance on a weekly basis, make sure you include this in your expense list. Also, don't forget any "free money" you might hand your kids when they go to the mall, out with a friend, or to the movies. Sometimes, it's those little extras that add up quickly, and if they aren't planned for they can cause other areas of the budget to be tight.

List Everything You Buy Each Week

Online purchases – Can I just be the first to admit I love shopping online? However, that can also be my downfall. Make sure that any purchases you would make online are also included in your budget. I buy a lot of household products online like toilet paper, paper towels, etc. If you do the same, those are items you want to make sure get included.

Listing out everything you are buying in a week will help you as you start assigning amounts to your budget. I know the tendency is to pretend that we don't buy that much, but it's actually more helpful at this stage to over-estimate items on your expense list. The longer your list of expenses, the more informed your decision will be when you start prioritizing your spending.

Day 6: Create a Weekly Expense List

Now that you have a good idea of what items need to be included in your Expense List, use the **Weekly Expense Chart** to organize your expenses. The goal is to list all of the items you buy on a weekly basis. Try to think of as many as you can right now, then walk away and come back to it in about an hour and see if you have any more to add to the list. Remember, the more detailed your Expense Chart, the better your budget will be in the long run! Once you have a list of expenses and amounts, try giving the items a priority from 1 to 5, with a 1 being not really important and a 5 being something that you can't live without.

Budgeting with Kids:

Ask you kids what they buy or spend money on in a typical week. This is a great conversation for the dinner

How to Make a Budget Work for You

table and might be a great time to also ask them what items you buy that they could live without.

If you don't already, be open with your kids about how much things cost. It's important for kids to understand that it takes money to run the lights in your home and the water in the sink and to put food on the table. Often, kids don't grasp that they are spending money on things that they don't see, so it's important to have these conversations to shape a healthy view of money in our kids.

Day 7

Create a Monthly Expense Chart

Documents You Will Need:

➢ **Monthly Expense Chart**

One of the biggest downfalls of most budgets is the failure to plan for less frequent expenses. Things like a mortgage or car payments are usually first on the list, but there are a lot of other monthly expenses that you want to make sure you're planning for. If you get paid on a weekly basis and you pay your car payment and house payment monthly, then you want to set aside enough money out of each paycheck to cover those expenses at the end of the month when they are due.

How to Create a Monthly Expense Chart

In my household, some of our biggest budget expenses are monthly. That means it's important to be planning for all of these expenses every time you receive a paycheck. That will help you ensure that you don't end up with bills at the end of the month that you can't pay. By prioritizing and planning for these larger monthly expenses, it will help you determine your weekly budget--or bi-weekly budget--depending on how frequently you are paid.

How to Make a Budget Work for You

Here are a few things you want to remember:

Shelter, transportation, and utilities – These are the major expenses in most households. Make sure you include your mortgage, rent, car payments, and monthly household utility bills such as the electric, water, gas, cable, internet, cell phone, and other bills you get each month.

Insurance – Some insurance plans allow you to pay monthly. Others may be annual or semi-annual. If you pay on a monthly basis, then you will want to add any insurance premiums to the list. Some insurance companies offer discounts for pre-paying on a semi-annual or annual basis. Once you have a solid budget, this might be a way to reduce your monthly spending-- by switching to a less frequent payment schedule.

Medical Bills – A lot of families budget monthly for medical bills and out-of-pocket treatments. If you have prescriptions you buy on a monthly basis, don't forget to add these to the list. Other treatments like physical therapy, eye exams, dentist visits, chiropractor visits, and other routine treatments should also be included.

Note: These are expenses that may occur on a regular basis, not medical bills for past surgeries or illnesses for which you owe. Those should be listed with your debts.

Childcare/Tuition – If you have kids in childcare or a private school, you may have monthly tuition expenses that need to be planned for. There may also be additional expenses associated with after school or extracurricular activities such as baseball, gymnastics, dance, or the gym that need to be planned for, as well.

Create a Monthly Expense Chart

This is just the beginning, to get you thinking through all of the things you need to pay for each month. These can sometimes be the most tricky expenses because if you are living paycheck to paycheck, it's important to set aside the money for these items before you spend it. That way you don't end up getting behind on these bills or going into debt if you can't pay them.

Day 7: Create a Monthly Expense List

Now that you have a good idea of what items need to be included, use the **Monthly Expense Chart** to organize your expenses. The goal is to list all of the items you spend money on each month. Once you have a list of expenses and amounts, try giving the items a number by number from 1 to 5, with 1 being not as important and a 5 being something that is extremely important to you.

Budgeting with Kids:

Sometimes kids don't realize all the things that we as parents pay for on a monthly basis. It is easy for kids to overlook the boring expenses like the newspaper or trash bill :) They also don't really understand the costs of utilities and how important and easy it can be to save money just by turning off the lights! If you have older kids, have them try to guess everything on your monthly expense list and then talk through all of these items with them. It will give them an appreciation for some of the little things they most likely take for granted.

Day 8

Plan for Yearly Expenses

Documents You Will Need:

> **Infrequent Expense Chart**

I cannot think of anything that can ruin a budget more than an unexpected "big" expense. I always recommend that you have a minimum $1,000-2,000 emergency fund for things you can't plan for. However, most of these "unexpected" items really aren't emergencies--they are failures to plan. It really isn't hard to plan for these yearly, semiannual, or infrequent expenses. The problem is that most of the time we just don't stop long enough to figure out what expenses we need to plan for.

It's easy to get so busy that we think we don't have time to create a budget, or a list of expenses, and those tasks can seem unimportant. If you are failing to plan, you are planning to fail, and it will take you more time to manage your money on the backend of your spending than it will to manage your money before you spend it! Taking time to plan will actually save you in the long run, but for most of us the hardest part is making the planning a priority. If you haven't already set aside some time, maybe take a few hours on a Saturday or Sunday to sit down and list out your expenses and create a budget. This will save you so much time once you have a plan in place.

Plan for Yearly Expenses

Plan for Yearly & Infrequent Expenses

Some of the most common infrequent expenses that we have in our household include car insurance, homeowners insurance, property taxes, car license plates, renewing a driver's license, vacations, Christmas gifts, end-of-the-year teachers' gifts, birthday presents, birthday parties, and taxes.

One of the most important things I can suggest is that you look over the last year of household expenses, either on your credit card or your bank statement, to determine what expenses you had that you will likely have again over the next year. Then take the amounts you need to save and divide it by 12, or by your typical paycheck interval.

For example, if you have a $600 insurance bill you pay each year, you would want to divide this by 12 to get the monthly amount you need to set back each month.

$600/12=$50 per month

If you get paid every other week, then you need to save the full amount and divide it by 26 (that's half the number of weeks in a year since you get paid every other week). Or if you get paid twice a month, divide by 24.

$600/26=$23.08

How to Make a Budget Work for You

If you could set back $23.08 out of each paycheck, then you would have enough money to make the $600 payment each year. If you are already a few months into the year, you may need to adjust the amount so that you have the money ready to go when the payment comes up. Then you can re-adjust after the first payment is made.

You can plan for all larger, infrequent expenses this way. All you need to do is start by listing the items you need to save for each year, divide the payment amounts by the number of paychecks you expect to receive, and that's your budget amount. You need to set back that specific amount out of each paycheck to avoid scrambling at the last minute to find the money.

By planning and preparing for larger, infrequent expenses, you can avoid these budget emergencies, and that will help you keep all of the other items in your budget on track each month.

Day 8: Create an Infrequent Expense List

Now that you have a good idea of what items need to be included, use the **Infrequent Expense Chart** to organize your expenses. The goal is to list all of the infrequent items that come up each year so that you can plan ahead and be better prepared to handle these expenses. Once you have a list of expenses and amounts, divide by 52 if you get paid weekly, 26 if you get paid every other week, 24 if you get paid twice a month, or 12 if you are paid monthly. The smaller amount is what you need to set back each paycheck to have the money available when your payment is due.

Plan for Yearly Expenses

Having the money set aside before the payment is due will help you keep the rest of your budget on track. This helps to avoid robbing one area to pay another and constantly feeling behind. We will talk about what to do if you don't have enough money in your budget to cover all of these infrequent expenses in a little bit.

Budgeting with Kids:

Start talking with your kids now about an expense coming up in the future. Maybe this is a new baseball bat for the spring season, or a birthday present for a sibling--something that they could easily work towards and save for. Explain the importance of thinking ahead and working hard now so that we have the money to buy the things in the future that we will need and want. Sometimes, a small item can be a great training exercise for kids. They can easily start saving now if you can help them set the goals and think about the importance of saving for future expenses.

Day 9

Plan for Personal Fun Money

I'm so excited about today's topic because it's one of my favorite aspects of budgeting. Now I should start off to say that if you are on an extremely tight budget, you might not have room to plan for "fun money." But if you can even afford $5 each, it really does make a difference in your attitude towards a budget.

Plan for Personal Fun Money

One of the things that always comes up when I am talking with someone about a budget is that typically one member of the household is more "controlling" with money than the other person. What happens is that one person wants tight restrictions and the other person feels smothered. I typically attribute most of this to the different spending personalities we already talked about. One of the best ways to control the urge to overspend is by allowing a little margin in your budget. I like to call this "fun money," but really it's a way to allow you a little freedom to have a few dollars that you can decide how to spend each week.

This does not have to be a lot of money. Maybe you can assign $5 to $10 per person each week, but that's enough money to allow them to get coffee with a friend or go out to lunch one day a week. Or maybe you can assign $25 each and that can be saved if you want to get your nails done every other week. It really doesn't

How to Make a Budget Work for You

matter what your "fun money" is spent on. It's completely up to you, and it can be ever changing depending on your needs or wants for the week or month. There is just one catch with fun money--it's just that. It's supposed to be fun!!! This is the margin that allows you to choose something you enjoy. You can save it up and buy something big or spend it each week, and no one can tell you what it can or can't be spent on :)

I have talked with a lot of couples who have gotten married and are trying to make a budget work, and one of the things that always comes up is something like this conversation:

"He wants to spend money on X, and well she wants to always do Z."

The idea with fun money is that you might not be able to do those things all the time, but you are given the freedom to make the decisions with at least a small portion of the budget. Like I said, it doesn't have to be a lot of money--for the most part, you should have your money budgeted. This is just your extra to have a little fun with each week. This small amount of freedom will also help you stay on track on other areas of your budget. For example, if you have a tight budget for eating out it might be a luxury to spend your fun money going to lunch with a friend, but it's your choice, and by having this small budget you can make those decisions and not feel as deprived as you might if you didn't have a little margin.

One last thing I want to mention: If you have expenses that are frequent, these should be planned for. For

Plan for Personal Fun Money

example, if you are going out to eat every Tuesday and Thursday, that should be in the budget. If you are getting your nails done every other week (rather than a once in a while splurge), it's much easier to account for these frequent expenses by assigning them their own budget category. Try to keep your fun money for the spur of the moment needs and wants that might not be provided for in your budget.

Day 9: Talk Over Your Fun Money Amount

We are taking a break from the tedious homework of making expense charts to enjoy a little chit-chat over fun money. I want you to take some time to talk over exactly what you might use your fun money for! Talk about what you think you might be able to afford depending on your income and budget. This will be different for each family, but try to make the amounts equal for each person so there isn't any resentment over the amount of spending for any party involved.

Budgeting with Kids:

If you have kids, an easy way to teach them to save is by giving them both spend money and save money. Try teaching them that you can save your "save money" towards a long-term goal (think college, vacations, or a car), and that your spending money is what you spend frequently. Let them go to the store once a month or once a week, depending on how much they have, and allow them to spend that money. If you encourage your kids to save everything, then by allowing them to pull out of savings each time they want to buy something, they really aren't learning the value of savings. So try helping them budget their money out into a part they can spend and a part they can save. We actually use

How to Make a Budget Work for You

three categories for our kids: giving, saving, and spending.

Day 10

Dividing Your Expenses Into Categories

Documents You Will Need:

- **Weekly Expense Worksheet**
- **Monthly Expense Worksheet**
- **Infrequent Expense Summary**
- **Category Summary Worksheet**

I hope you took the time to complete the homework over the last few days, because today we are going to start using the worksheets that you should have already created, and today's tasks will be a lot less time-consuming if you have already completed the **Weekly Expense Worksheet,** the **Monthly Expense Worksheet,** and the **Infrequent Expense Summary.**

How to Divide Your Expenses Into Categories

Today's task is to divide your expenses into categories. How I want you to start is by going through the three worksheets listed above and deciding if items can be grouped together. I do want to caution you that the more you group things, the more discipline you have to have. But the tighter your budget, the more division you may want in order to ensure you aren't over spending and that you have money left for the most important items.

How to Make a Budget Work for You

Some of the major categories you should have include:

- ➢ **Groceries**: food, beverages, meats, lunch items, breakfast cereals, milk, bread, etc.)
- ➢ **Personal Care Items**: deodorant, toothpaste, toothbrushes, pads, tampons, shampoo, styling products, etc.)
- ➢ **Household Cleaning Items**: trash bags, cleaning supplies, paper towels
- ➢ **Clothing**: You can put the family together, or break this out by person.

Other items will include your mortgage, car payments insurance, medical expenses (co-pays, prescriptions, etc.), haircuts, vacation savings, Christmas gift savings, and tuition.

The important thing is to start summarizing your detailed worksheets into more general budget categories. Remember, right now you aren't assigning values to each category--we are just trying to make sure we are planning for all the expenses that come up in a year.

As you combine Expense Summary items into categories, list the total you estimate you spend on that category. This will just give you an idea of what you have been spending so that you can be realistic when you start

Dividing Your Expenses into Categories

setting those budget amounts. Remember, our income will be the driving factor in our budget. We can't spend more than we have, so our budget category amounts will be set by the income we bring in and priority--not by the amount we want to spend, but an amount that's practical for each category in our budget.

Day 10: Create your Category Summary

Pull out your Weekly, Monthly and Infrequent Expense summary charts and start combining individual items into more general categories. You will need to list the sum of the items in that category so that you know how much you typically spend on those items per paycheck. Then give the category an overall importance. As you work through the **Category Summary Worksheet**, start crossing items off the Weekly, Monthly, and Infrequent charts until all items have been added to your **Category Summary Worksheet**. This should ensure that all items you typically buy are covered in your **Category Summary Worksheet**.

Budgeting with Kids:

We try really hard to keep things simple for our kids so that it's easy for them to understand. Our kids are little, so we stick to just three categories with them: Spend, Save, and Give. If you have older kids you might want to consider having them pay for their own movies, or maybe their own school lunches when they don't take their lunch from home. Or maybe you want them to have their own clothing budget. As kids get older, the number of categories they can manage will grow, so keep it simple for little ones and slowly add categories as your kids grow up.

Day 11

Prioritize Your Budget Categories

Documents You Will Need:

> **Category Summary Worksheet**

Today is all about how to prioritize your categories. Something to keep in mind is that while you have (hopefully) made a huge list of categories, there may or may not be enough room in your budget for all of your categories, so we're going to talk about the best way to handle this situation today.

How to Prioritize Your Categories

One of the most common problems in a budget is that you have more expenses going out than the income you have coming in. While this isn't really the fun part to talk about, this is the reality for most people. If you're sitting down to make a budget, there's a good chance you're going to discover that your spending outweighs your income. Here are a few different ways you can handle the situation:

Reduce the Budget Amount of Each Category - One way to handle this situation is by reducing the budget amount of each category until your total of all your budget categories equals your weekly or monthly income. This can be tricky because some categories like eating out or entertainment might not be as important

How to Make a Budget Work for You

as groceries. Also, some categories aren't negotiable. For example, you can't choose to only pay 50% of your water or electric bills, so fixed amounts also create problems.

Eliminate Categories Completely – This is also another option. You could go through your list of categories and just get rid of categories you want to do without. In reality, you probably need to do a little category clean up, but you don't want to completely eliminate categories. There may be categories that don't get a weekly or monthly allotment, but you can choose to have these be flexible accounts, which means that when you have additional income (bonuses, overtime pay, etc.), you can add to these categories out of the overflow or extra income you have coming in. This is a great way to handle jobs that have commission or infrequent payments. For example, our vacation fund isn't building with each paycheck, but we add to it out of my husband's quarterly bonuses. Since it's not a necessity, it doesn't get priority in our budget.

Prioritize Your Categories – This is my preferred method for balancing income and expenses. Basically, the idea is that you sit down and ask yourself, "If I had only enough money to do one budget category, which one is the most important" You want to start numbering your categories in order starting, with 1 and going as high as your number of categories. This is how you determine your priority of spending. After you have given each category a priority number, you can then play with the amounts allotted to each category in order to make things balance. There may also be categories you choose to eliminate because you can live without them or categories that become flexible,

Prioritize Your Budget Categories

meaning you only add to them when you have additional income.

Day 11: Giving Order to Your Categories

Pull out your **Category Summary Worksheet** from yesterday and start placing numbers to the left of each category. You want to start with 1, then go up as far as you need until all of your categories have a number. Remember that the categories at the end of the worksheet may or may not make it into the budget, so be sure to choose the most practical items like food, shelter, and utilities first. Once we have completed the **Income Planning Worksheet**, we will begin assigning values to each category. These values are still flexible. The more you are willing to adjust the value of each budget category, the more categories will fit in your budget. Just remember that long-term practicality is our goal. You can't have one hundred categories with $5 each because it's probably not practical to your family's needs. A well-balanced budget accounts and accurately plans for our needs in a realistic manner.

The freedom in budgeting comes from accurately planning for needs so you aren't forced to decide if you are going to overspend or buy groceries. We want to cover the most basic expenses first by telling our money where to go rather than letting our money control us.

Budgeting with Kids:

Priorities can be a hard concept for kids to grasp. Have you ever been to Wal-Mart or Target with a child who asks for every item they see? Kids often don't grasp the idea that they can't just buy every item all at once.

How to Make a Budget Work for You

One way we teach our kids priorities is by allowing them to earn money through chores. When they ask for an item, I tell them we can add it to their Wish List. This is a list of items they want and are saving for. When they have enough money in their spend account to buy an item on their Wish List, they get to choose which item they want. Our kids quickly figured out that they couldn't have every item they asked for and that they had to choose their priorities carefully. It's been fascinating to watch them learn to not only save their money but prioritize their spending. It's also interesting to watch the different personality types handle money, even at a young age.

Day 12

Make a List of All Your Income

Documents You Will Need:

➢ **Income Planning Worksheet**

Now that we have spent a lot of time talking about spending habits, discussing categories, and prioritizing needs, it's time to tackle the other side of the equation. There are two parts in every budget--the expenses (spending/saving) and the income. Obviously, the more money you have coming in, the more you have going into savings and spending categories. If you find your budget isn't balancing, you can either start cutting portions of your spending/saving categories or work to increase your income.

How to Summarize Your Income

The first thing we need to talk about is different kinds of income. There are several different types of income that will affect the flexibility of your budget. Because no families' income streams are the same, this is personal. This is the first part of creating your own personal budget. How your categories and budget work will be based on your personal income streams.

Fixed Income – If you have a regular eight-to-five salaried job in which you get paid every two weeks, and your check is always the same amount, you probably have the easiest type of income to budget. This fixed income is predictable. You get the same amount each time you get paid, and it's consistent in the sense that you work the same amount of hours each week and it's not commission based.

Flexible Income – In today's work environments, we see a lot of flexible income models. These are people who have part salary, part commission jobs, jobs that are entirely commission-based, and hourly jobs that might vary in hours each week. The idea with the flexible income stream is that you never really know how much your check will be. You may have a small fixed amount (or base salary) then additional commissions or hourly incentives that are a little harder to plan for. Knowing how much income you have coming in that is fixed versus flexible is essential when planning your budget.

Supplemental Income – One of the best ways to increase your budgeting ability or to fund budget categories that might not fall within your standard weekly budget is through supplemental income. These are income streams that are somewhat random in nature. It might be an on-the-side home business, a second business you run from your home, contract work you do for a friend every summer, or other ways you and your family earn money. Typically, supplemental income is the easiest and quickest way to add to your overall income, and it's a great way to fund categories that might not fall within the normal family budget. The problem with supplemental income is that it's unpredictable in nature. Most supplemental income can't be planned for, so we will discuss how to handle this income when you begin planning your budget.

Make a List of All Your Income

Day 12: Defining Your Income

Today's task is to start defining your income. You should download and print the **Income Planning Worksheet** and list every source of income you can think of. Start by working your way through the list above. List your fixed income, the flexible income, and the supplemental income streams you have each year. Then you want to do your best to estimate the amount of income coming in through each income stream. The last task will be defining the income streams as fixed, flexible and supplemental. That's going to help us put our budget together in a way that's organized and makes sense.

Important: Pay attention to the difference between Gross Income and Net Income. If you have a fixed salary income, the amount you are paid each month (before taxes, insurance, retirement, etc.) is Gross Income. The amount you actually receive in your check is your Net Income. I prefer to budget on the Gross Income and to create categories for each item coming out of my check, so I would have categories for IRA, health insurance, taxes, etc. The only reason this is important is it allows you to see the actual amount you are spending on these items and where your money is actually going. If you want to budget based off your Gross Income, list the gross amount on your planning worksheet and make sure you include all categories that are coming out of your check so that it balances. If you want to budget off the net income (what you actually bring home), make sure you list the net amount. Confusing the two might make things complicated later on when your budget doesn't balance.

How to Make a Budget Work for You

Budgeting with Kids:

This is a great time to talk with your kids about the different ways they can earn money. I really believe in having my kids do "chores" because they are a part of the household. Then I also like to pay them to do other tasks in order for them to learn the value of working for their money. I really believe kids can make smarter decisions about the things they buy when they have worked hard for the money in their hands, so I'm a big proponent of giving kids opportunities to earn even from a young age. Take some time to talk with your kids about opportunities that they have to earn money. Maybe it's walking a neighbor's dog, having a paper route, or babysitting for a friend or younger sibling. If you have little ones, consider paying them to fold towels, empty the dishwasher, dust the house, vacuum, or sweep and mop. The list of ideas will obviously depend on your own family and financial situation, but it's a great time to start encouraging your kids to think of ways they can earn supplemental, flexible, and fixed income.

Day 13

Combine Your Income and Expenses

Documents You Will Need:

- ➢ **Income Planning Worksheet**
- ➢ **Category Summary Worksheet**
- ➢ **Budget Planning Worksheet**

Today we are going to talk about combining your income and expenses into one budget that works together. You see, I could sit here for days and come up with long lists of items I would like to have in my budget, but the reality is that I can only spend as much as I make. That's the point of a budget: to help us pay down debt and work to live within our means. If you find your budget is tight, then you may want to start looking for other ways to increase your income, which will in turn give you more flexibility within your budget.

Combining Income and Expenses

Your income and your budget are basically one in the same. I don't believe in going into debt for regular everyday expenses. In fact, one of my goals is to provide you with the resources to live on less so that you can pay down debt you may have accumulated through school loans, credit cards, and other means. When you are creating your personal budget, your

How to Make a Budget Work for You

income less your budget categories will always equal zero.

One of the most common questions I get when I talk about a zero-based budget (which means, everything that comes in gets "spent" somewhere) is that people start to worry that if they spend all of their money, they won't have any savings. This would be true if you failed to create a "savings" category in your budget. Just because you are budgeting every dollar of your income does not mean that you are not saving and preparing for the future. In fact, I've been encouraging you to save and plan and prepare for the future so that you aren't hit with unexpected expenses, which can be a huge budget buster!

When you start prioritizing and listing your expenses and budget categories, I want you to consider putting savings at the top of the list. Our personal budget includes categories for taxes, IRA (a form of savings), actual savings, emergency accounts, insurance, and other priorities towards the top of the list. Then we move into things like food and groceries, gas, household items, car savings, etc. Because we have categories for things like savings, our emergency fund, retirement, and even items that we don't make payments on like a house savings fund and car savings fund, we are planning and preparing for these big expenses all while still working towards our savings and retirement goals. The idea here is that just because it's a budget category, it might not be a spending category. You need to make it a priority to pay yourself and your savings accounts out of each paycheck so that you aren't living month to month without savings.

Combine Your Income and Expenses

I know that if you're already living from paycheck to paycheck, it can be hard to even think of saving money first, but I want to challenge you to even set aside a little bit out of each paycheck. This might be $10, $20, $100 or more depending on where you are, and it might be a goal of yours to be able to save more once you pay down debt. I really believe that nothing brings a budget crashing down faster than emergencies and unplanned expenses. If you don't currently have any savings, try saving towards an emergency fund of $1000 to start with. Then move to three months' worth of expenses. These are small goals that will get you started towards the path of savings and help you have a little breathing room when those emergencies in life come up.

Day 13: How to Combine Your Income & Expenses

Now that you have your **Income Planning Worksheet** and your **Category Summary Worksheet**, we are ready to start combining the two worksheets to create your personal budget. Today, we will be working with the **Budget Planning Worksheet**!

The first thing you want to do is bring everything down to equal playing fields. Determine the term you want to use for your budget. Typically, this should coincide with your payment frequency. If you are paid every other week, it makes sense to work on a two-week budget. If you get paid monthly, then you can work a monthly budget. Others may receive weekly checks, and you will want to work on a weekly budget.

If your income is all flexible and you don't get paid at consistent intervals, then let me suggest a monthly

How to Make a Budget Work for You

budget. This is the easiest way to plan since most bills/expenses occur monthly.

Start by listing all your income streams in the order of consistency (fixed, flexible, and then supplemental). List the income amount based on the term you want to use for your budget. So if you make $40,000 a year, and you want to work on a 2 week budget, divide $40,000 by 26 so that your worksheet lists the amount of income coming in during each budget term (or two weeks, in this example).

Next, list your budget categories, starting with the most important first, then the next most important, etc. You should have done some of this in the **Category Summary Worksheet** when you gave each item a number. If you followed all the steps in that section, you can start with Item 1, then move through 2, 3, and so on. Make sure you don't forget to add in personal savings or your emergency fund! Also, remember that if you budget off the gross income, then you need to have a category for each item that's taken out of your paycheck so that things balance in the end.

IMPORTANT: Do not list your category amounts, yet. We'll be talking more about the category amounts before we get to this step.

Once you have your income and expenses listed on this chart, you will start to see how your budget is going to line out. We will be saving assigning values until tomorrow, but you could quickly go down your budget and see about how far you get with your income that you have currently.

Combine Your Income and Expenses

Budgeting with Kids:

If you have older children, take time to talk with your kids about the expenses they have on a daily basis. It's important not necessarily as kids are little, but as they reach teenage years, that they understand even the basic costs of living in a home. Most kids understand a mortgage, but as we are training and preparing our kids to leave home one day, we also want to make sure that we give them the understanding of all the bills and expense that living on your own brings. I'll never forget moving out of my parents' home and seeing the bill for the trash truck and recycling one day :) I just never even thought about paying for items like that before, yet they're a necessary part of our monthly budget now.

Day 14

Assigning Amounts to Each Category

Documents You Will Need:

- **Budget Planning Worksheet**
- **Category Summary Worksheet**

Yesterday, we got a good start on the **Budget Planning Worksheet.** Today we are going to finish this up by assigning amounts to each category. Hopefully you listed all your income sources and your categories in order of priority. Now we're ready to discuss how to assign values to each category.

Assigning Amounts to Each Category

The goal for today is to start balancing your budget. There's one main principle that we want to abide by: your spending cannot be greater than your income.

Hopefully you spent some time thinking about the priority of your categories. We are going to start at the top of our list and work down in order. I would suggest using a pencil for this part since you might need to adjust amounts as you get further down your worksheet. For each category, you will want to look back over your **Category Summary Worksheet** to see how much money you typically spend on that category, then decide what a realistic amount is for your new budget.

How to Make a Budget Work for You

Some categories will be fixed (like a mortgage or car payment). Others, like eating out, may be more flexible. Keep in mind that what you have been spending in the past on eating out may not be what you can actually afford. This is the time to think about lifestyle changes that need to be made to make your budget work in all aspects. Take some time to talk over each category with your spouse or family members as you determine a realistic amount for each category.

Start with the first category and assign an amount, then deduct this amount from your Sum of Income and write down the remaining amount of income. You can continue going as far down your worksheet as you have money remaining. When you run out of income you won't be able to fund any additional categories. This is the time you're most likely going to start looking back over your categories and starting to make some compromises. You may decide that a category is more important than another, or that you don't need as much as you originally thought in some categories.

Something important to remember is that if your income is flexible or supplemental, you may not make it as far each month as you think. If all of your income is flexible, you want to go in order each month and fund each budget category as the money comes in. That means you're going to start with savings, mortgage, food, lights, water, etc. The basic necessities get funded first each month, then as additional income comes in, you can continue down your list.

If your income is inconsistent--meaning that you get big payouts every few months, then nothing in between--try

Assigning Amounts to Each Category

estimating what you can live off of each month. When you get a big payout, fund two to three months of necessities before moving on to other categories. That way you have the money waiting to cover those months in between when you might not see a paycheck.

Day 14: How to Assign Amounts to Categories

Start with the first category listed on your **Budget Planning Worksheet** and assign the amount you believe you need for that category (remember to keep the time period of your budget in mind). Then deduct the amount from your total income and list the income remaining.

When you move to the next category, assign an amount and deduct the amount from the income remaining in the row above it. This will give you a running total of how much money is left. It also helps you to visually see how many categories you can cover with your income.

I suggest using a pencil because when you get to $0 in income remaining, you may find you have categories that are important to you that aren't funded. You can handle this either by adjusting some of the categories above this point in the budget or by making these supplemental categories, meaning that when you receive additional income, you choose to fund these categories the additional income. If that's your plan, go ahead and add an amount to those categories so that you have an idea of how much you need to fund each of these categories.

How to Make a Budget Work for You

An example of supplemental categories in our budget might be vacation savings or Christmas gifts. You can work extra jobs, have a garage sale, house sit, or babysit for a friend to earn some extra money. When you earn extra money, you can add that to these supplemental categories to help meet all of your goals.

Remember: You may not be able to cover everything on your category list. Just because it's listed in your categories does not mean that you get to spend money there; that's why we spent some time prioritizing. The only way to add categories is by adding income or reducing other categories. This is the entire point of a budget--to make you think and prioritize. It also helps you to avoid overspending in unnecessary areas, leaving you with a rent or mortgage payment that you can't fund at the end of the month. By setting priorities, you are taking care of the most important needs for you and your family first and planning and preparing for other expenses.

Budgeting with Kids:

Setting priorities can be hard. Take some time to talk with your kids about the priorities you and your family have. If you are having to sacrifice in some areas in order to be prepared for other areas, make sure you discuss with your kids not only the need to sacrifice but the benefits of it, as well. Help them see the big picture: that living within your means is the long-term answer to getting out of debt and living better on less! A lot of times, kids don't understand the consequences of overspending. They don't really understand the difference between buying an item you can afford and buying an item on a credit card. Remember to keep

Assigning Amounts to Each Category

your budget in the center of your conversations, because kids can learn so much from these everyday life experiences--lessons that will help them for years to come!

Day 15

Handling Additional Categories

Now that you have worked through the **Budget Planning Worksheet**, there is a good chance that you got to the end of your income and still had a significant number of categories left unfunded. Today we are going to talk about how to handle these remaining categories.

How to Handle Additional Categories

One of the most sobering realities about a budget is that you may or may not be able to afford everything that you have been buying. If you have been struggling to make ends meet and you have been searching for money at the end of each month, there is a good chance you were overspending. So the fact that you didn't have enough income to cover all your categories should serve as a means of bringing things back into balance. Here are a few steps you can take if you don't have enough income to cover all your categories.

Get realistic - Take a look back over all your categories. Each time you look over your categories, try to imagine what you could realistically live with in each category. Remember that you're going to have to stick to whatever you decide, so make your decisions wisely. You may also need to get realistic about the categories

Handling Additional Categories

remaining--maybe you can eliminate some of the remaining categories.

Reduce other budget categories - I'll never forget the reason I started using coupons. We were having a "budget meeting," and our household food expenses were going up. Gas was $4 a gallon, and my husband wanted to reduce the clothing budget so that we could add more to the food budget. I knew there had to be a better way, so I decided to find a way to make my food budget work even with the increases in prices. When I started getting creative, using a meal plan and shopping with coupons, we were able to make some of our budget categories work on less than we thought.

Look for ways to increase your income – Even if you can find a small part-time job, take on a job on the weekends, keep some other kids in your home one or two days a week, or start your own at-home business, you can use that increased income to cover additional categories that might not be funded out of your current income. So get creative and start thinking of ways that you can earn extra money. I remember when just earning $20 a week was a huge difference for me because it allowed my husband and I each to have about $10 per week in "fun money" that we could spend wherever we wanted! There was also a time I took food surveys at our local college to earn $40 Wal-Mart gift cards. I used these to buy groceries and help keep our budget in line. Sometimes it doesn't take much money to give you flexibility and breathing room in your budget.

Get Creative - You might need to take some time to stop and think of other ways you could accomplish the same goals. For example, there are some great

How to Make a Budget Work for You

household ideas for how to save money on cleaning supplies on Pinterest. You could also switch to reusable cloths instead of paper towels, or cut out your cable/satellite and get Netflix or Sling. There are a lot of ways to reduce the amount you are currently spending, so don't get stuck on what you spent last month, get creative and see how much you can save next month!

Evaluate, Evaluate, Evaluate - Your budget doesn't have to stay static over the next year. You can re-evaluate every month at the beginning of the month so that if you find that you're not spending as much as you anticipated in a few of your categories, you will have more flexibility to add back in some of the categories you had left over. Remember that you probably won't get your budget exactly right on the first try, so evaluating every month for the first three to four months will help you come up with a more realistic budget.

Day 15: How to Handle Additional Categories

We're going to take a break from the in-depth homework today, and I just want you to make a simple list of five ways you can save and five ways you can earn.

You may discover that just calling your cable/internet provider could reduce your bill by $5-$10 a month or more. You might save money on gas by only doing errands once per week. The list of ideas could go on forever, so think of five ways you could save money and write them down (remember these are ways you can

Handling Additional Categories

save in *addition* to the budget amounts you have already set).

Earning money might seem a little trickier, but remember it doesn't have to be a lot of money. You can get online on sites like Fivrr.com and earn $5 for doing simple tasks, or you could set out to start your own baking business or at-home business. Set realistic and simple goals of how much you want to earn. Remember that just $25-$50 a week can make a huge difference in most people's budgets, so don't set your goals too high to start with and you'll be more encouraged to accomplish these goals.

The next step is to determine what categories you could cover if you did any of these items. For example, if you could babysit for a friend one day a week, you might be able to fund a category that was important to you and that might be the motivation you need to put up a message on Facebook letting your friends know you're willing to babysit at your home on Mondays!

The ideas are limitless. Don't get tied into my suggestions; think of ideas and situations that fit within your family lifestyle! This is your budget, and you can make it work if you set your mind to it.

Budgeting with Kids:

If you have older kids, one way to handle additional categories that involve your kids is by making them responsible for earning their own money. If you have teenagers, they may be able to get a job or start babysitting to pay for gas money, car insurance, or even

How to Make a Budget Work for You

just their own lunch money. Other ideas would include having your kids pay for their own Friday night entertainment money, summer camps, sports fees, etc.

Day 16

How to Handle Additional Income

Documents You Will Need:

➢ Budget Planning Worksheet

Yesterday's topic on how to handle additional categories was not nearly as fun as today's topic: How to handle additional income! This is the problem we all wish we had, but the truth is sometimes "additional income" doesn't mean excess income.

How to Handle Additional Income

There are two types of additional income. The first would be what I've called previously "flexible income" or "supplementary income." This is income you need to make your budget work, and it's somewhat planned, but the exact amount wasn't known ahead of time. The second type of income is excess income, meaning you weren't planning on it and you don't need it to make your budget work, so you have a lot more flexibility with this type of income.

Supplementary Income - If you receive income to help supplement your budget, maybe from doing odd jobs, then you want to start by going down your **Budget Planning Worksheet** to see what the first unfunded or partially unfunded category is. You can add enough to that budget category to fund the category then move on to the next category and continue down the list until you run out of money. Or, you can choose to put the money all in one category if you don't expect additional income for a while. You may decide that you want to put two to three weeks' or months' worth in a category that's important to you in order to plan ahead for the future. This is completely fine so long as all of your major necessities and bills are taken care of first.

Excess Income - One of the most dangerous things that can happen to your budget is you receive unexpected money and you just blow it! :) That can be fun at first, but I really believe you should always have a plan, even if the plan is to spend the money on something fun. The idea is that you don't want to get into a binge type mentality, where you skimp and scrape by on a tight budget then all the sudden you go 180 degrees the other way and just spend a bunch of money that was unexpected. I really want to encourage you to stop and think about what you're spending your money on before you make a purchase, no matter what the purchase or where the money came from.

If you get unexpected money, sit down and make a Wish List. This could have things you want, things you need, something just fun for the family--it really doesn't matter-- the point is that you take time and you plan. You're staying in control of your money no matter what, not letting your money turn around and control you! There's more freedom and more flexibility long-term when you make planned, thought-out decisions with your finances!

Day 16: Dream Big

Today we are going to take a few moments to dream big. Write down three things you would like to have. These might be things you want to afford once you're out of debt. Maybe it's a family vacation to Disney World or a new car. Whatever the items are, just write them down. Sometimes dreaming big can help you keep your goals in perspective when the going gets tough. Then when you have excess money, go back to those goals. If these are items you still think are important, you might want to consider saving the money towards one of these special dreams. You might find you reach your dreams faster than you ever imagined!

Budgeting with Kids:

This is a great time to talk about your dreams with your kids. Help them catch the vision that being disciplined with money now will help you accomplish goals you have as a family to pay off debt, buy a house, go on vacation, and so much more! Remind them that sacrifice in the little things now might means you can have more opportunities to do some of the things on your and their Wish Lists in the future!

Day 17

Determine Cash & Set-Back Categories

Documents You Will Need:

> **Budget Planning Worksheet**

One of the last steps to finalizing your budget is determining your cash and set-back categories. One of the most important things to remember about a budget is that every dollar is spent before the month begins, so you know exactly how much you have to spend on groceries, gas, etc. The key is that you can't overspend. If you run out of money in that budget category, you have to stop spending and wait for the next budget time-period to make a purchase. This is the part of running on a budget that takes the most discipline, but it's also where you will see the most results.

How to Determine Cash & Set Back Categories

We work with three different types of budget accounts in our home, and I thought I would share these with you. I really believe that nothing helps you keep your budget in check better than using cash for everyday expenses. I know, I know--I have heard all the excuses, and honestly I've made them all myself, too, but every time we get behind on our budget, nothing brings us back faster than switching to cash!

How to Make a Budget Work for You

There are three different types of accounts you can use. I'm going to explain them here and give you a few examples:

Cash Accounts - Cash is so great because it allows you to physically see how much money is left in each budget category. You can use envelopes to keep your categories and money separated, or you can use paper clips and Post-It Notes in your wallet :) It doesn't have to be elaborate, but I promise you that using cash on items like groceries, health and beauty items, household items (think anything you buy at Wal-Mart or Target) will help you save money because it makes you think twice about every item that goes in your cart. We also use cash for lunch money, fun money and entertainment.

Checking Accounts - There are a lot of items in our budget that don't really make sense for cash. Most of these include tithe money, giving, and household bills like your mortgage, water, electric, and car payments. These items are monthly expenses, but you typically pay them online or by check and it doesn't make sense to get the money out and send cash in the mail :) So, the money from these accounts goes into our checking account each month, then we use a spreadsheet or online program to track the money in the checking account. This ensures that we have the money we need when the bills come due. It's important to keep in mind that you can't spend this money on something else. The money in your checking account should all be allotted to a specific category in your budget.

Set-Back Accounts - Some of your budget categories may be for longer term savings periods. If you have an

Determine Cash & Set-Back Categories

emergency fund, savings fund, car savings (if your car is paid off), property taxes, or other long-term items, then you can set this money aside in a savings account. This allows you to keep the money separate and save it for the time when you need the money. This is important if you tend to overspend. You don't want this money to be tapped into each week or month, so you want to put in a separate savings account where it can earn a low rate of interest and be safe from your debit card :) Remember to keep this money where you can get to it easily.--you may need this money during the year, but it's just not a part of your weekly or monthly expenses.

Day 17: Determine your Category Types

Take out your **Budget Planning Worksheet** and go through each category. List the category type for that category. At the end, summarize each type. This will tell you how much money goes into your checking account, how much money goes into your savings, and how much you need to get out in cash each pay period. Remember, if you have flexible income, your cash and set-back accounts work just like your income. As it comes in and you fund each category, you put the money where it needs to be based on the category type.

Budgeting with Kids:

Little kids and big kids alike can learn the value of savings. You might not go to the extent of telling your kids what a set-back account is, but it's easy with just the Save, Spend, and Give method to teach your kids to set back those savings for long-term goals. Most local banks offer child savings accounts. These typically only

How to Make a Budget Work for You

take a $5 minimum to open, and it's a great way to teach kids the importance of setting that money aside and not touching it for a long time. You can let your kids put their money in three envelopes or banks (Spend, Save, and Give). Then they can take the save money to the bank every month or few months and add this to their savings account. It's a simple way to teach the concept of cash vs. set-back accounts, even for little ones.

Day 18

Managing Your Budget on a Daily Basis

Documents You Will Need:

- ➢ **Budget Planning Worksheet**
- ➢ **Budget Spreadsheet**

Now that you've created your budget, it's time to figure out how you're going to manage all the day-to-day expenses. To be honest, you can make this as simple or as complex as you wish, but the easier your tracking process, the more likely your budget will work for you long-term.

How to Manage Your Budget

There are several different methods for managing your budget. What you need is a basic list of all the categories in your budget, then you'll start fresh one month, or at the beginning of a pay period, and add the amount for each budget category to your list. You can use a paper list, an Excel spreadsheet, or an online program like Every Dollar. This is a free app from the Dave Ramsey group, which is excellent!

I recommend sticking with a spreadsheet or the Every Dollar app online. This is actually my favorite because it allows you to have an app on your iPhone or Android device so that you always have access to your budget and also use the computer interface to set things up and

How to Make a Budget Work for You

track expenses. An app is extremely useful when you have more than one person using the same budget.

	A	B	C
1			
	Budget Categories	Category 1	Category 2
2	**Current Value**	**225.00**	**0.00**
3	Starting Value	200.00	
4	Expense	-25.00	
5	Expense	-50.00	
6	Expense	-100.00	
7	Add Money	200.00	
8			

Budget Spreadsheet

I set up a quick spreadsheet to give you some idea of how to get started. You can **download this basic Excel document from my website.**

If you are just starting out, it's a good idea to put your budget on paper or in a spreadsheet first then transfer those amounts into the app for your daily tracking.

You will want to start by listing all your budget categories along the top row. Then, on the third row, list the starting value of your budget. You can then list each expense and deduct it from the right category. I just use a negative sign (-) when deducting and the sum, or current value of the budget, as shown on Row 2. When you reach a new pay period and you need to

Managing Your Budget on a Daily Basis

add money, just insert a new row and add money to each category according to your **Budget Planning Worksheet**. You can also take out cash that just gets deducted from the categories.

Remember, with this method you can do multiple categories at once. So if you need to take $50 from gas and $10 from car savings for some reason, you can just put it on one row then list -$50 under the gas category and -$10 under car savings.

The same thing works when you are taking out cash. Do one withdrawal from your checking account and list all the amounts under each category. You may show a $0 balance in food, but that category is cash, so it's in your wallet and you can easily count how much you have.

I also highly recommend the Envelope Budgeting System online. This allows you to create "online" envelopes and works basically the same way the spreadsheet does.

If you are using the Every Dollar app or the Envelope Budgeting system online, here's how you can get started:

Step 1 – Set up an "electronic envelope" for each category you have.

Step 2 – Every time you get paid, you add the specific amounts from your **Budget Planning Worksheet** to each envelope

How to Make a Budget Work for You

Step 3 – Each time you make a purchase, you must add this to the app and deduct the purchase amount from the correct envelope(s)--this isn't done automatically, so you have to be disciplined, but that should help you think twice before spending.

Step 4 – When the envelope is empty, stop spending.

Step 5 – When you get paid or take out cash, you can either add or subtract money from your electronic envelopes accordingly.

The advantages to this online system is that you can have multiple people accessing the budget at once. You can also have access on the go, meaning you can put your purchases in as you make them. I think using a combination of the online budgeting with envelopes and actual cash accounts works best. Anything that's classified as a set-back account or a checking account will be great for online management. Anything classified as a cash account should be taken out in cash (just deduct the amount you take out from your budget category), which should be kept the cash in your wallet.

Day 18: Set up Your Budget Management System

Now is a great time to determine how you want to manage your budget and get started! Transfer your budget categories from your **Budget Planning Worksheet** to your spreadsheet or set up your electronic envelopes to get started! Then just enter your initial values and start tracking your purchases.

Managing Your Budget on a Daily Basis

Budgeting with Kids:

You can set up "categories" or "envelopes" for your kids even if you are using the simple Spend, Save, Give method. Just set up three envelopes, or three separate piggy banks, and allow kids to divide up their money each time they earn something. Encourage them to add money to each envelope or bank every time they get money. You might want to set specific percentages if you have older kids, or if you have little kids, just encourage them to divide it up. This will start to teach the principles of budgeting your money when you get it, rather than waiting till you're ready to spend to determine how much you should spend.

If your older kids have electronic devices and you want to teach them how to use a checking account, you can also help them use an app like the Every Dollar App to give every dollar in their checking account a category and help them understand how to manage a budget electronically.

Day 19

Tracking Your Expenses Daily

Now that you have your budget set up and you've determined what categories you need and how much to assign to each category, the next step is figuring out how you are going to track your expenses on a daily basis.

How to Track Your Expenses Daily

You have several options for tracking your expenses. This will somewhat depend on the method you choose for managing your budget. I wanted to give you a few ideas on how to work this on a daily basis.

Use Cash – Can I just be the first to tell you that if you use cash, it's the easiest way to manage your budget categories. Just divide your cash into different envelopes and take the money out as you need it. This is the simplest way to manage your money because it doesn't require tracking your purchases. When the money is gone, you can stop spending. This is actually my husband's reason for using cash--he doesn't like tracking a lot of little expenses and trying to enter everything into our budget spreadsheet, so he prefers to use cash for everyday purchases to avoid the extra work. Remember, the simpler you make your budgeting system, the easier it will be to stick to it long-term.

How to Make a Budget Work for You

Keep your receipts – For anything that's not a cash account, I keep my receipts in my wallet, and we have a basket at home on our office desk where they go. Then it is easy to sit down and take time to put these receipts into the **Budget Spreadsheet** or program. It's important that you know how much you are spending out of each budget, so this is one of the simplest ways for me to keep track of my spending from categories that aren't taken out in cash.

Use a check register – This is a little time consuming for me, but if you're really detailed you might like this option. You can use a check register to write down all of your purchases, which category they should come out of, and the amount. Then you can go through your check register and enter your expenses into your budget.

Use an app on the go – If you choose to use an online envelope management system like Every Dollar or a program that has a mobile app, you can enter your expenses as you go. The only thing you have to be careful of is forgetting to enter something. I'd make sure you set a time once a week to go over your credit card statement and checking account statement online to make sure you didn't miss something. If you forget to put in a purchase, you could easily overspend in that budget category, so make sure you keep a careful list of what you're buying.

There are several companies that offer automatic downloads from your checking account and credit cards; however, I find these systems are only reporting, and they don't require the active involvement in your budget on a daily basis that entering your receipts manually does. Sometimes, seeing exactly how much

Tracking Your Expenses Daily

you have spent and on what is the first step to finding the discipline to stick to your budget. It's easy to overspend when you aren't tracking your spending habits frequently.

Day 19: Determine How You Will Track Expenses

Think through which method will work best for you. You might decide that even though you prefer a spreadsheet system, having the ability to enter receipts and expenses from your mobile device is the convenience you need. It's not too late to set up an online budget that gives you access regardless of where you are. There really is no right or wrong way to manage your budget. The important thing is that you have an easy method that allows you to track your expenses daily.

Budgeting with Kids:

Using cash and envelopes for kids makes tracking spending really easy. This is the easiest method for kids to grasp because they can start to understand the principle that when the money is gone, it's gone. If you choose to get your kids a savings account, you can use a check register to help them keep the balance. I would recommend only putting "save" money in your savings account to keep things simple. Then all you have to track is the balance to know the value of the Save category.

Day 20

Communicate Consistently

Today we are going to talk about one of the most important factors that will affect the success of your budget. You can tell a lot about your finances and the success of your budget based on the level of communication involved in your finances.

How to Communicate Consistently

I know that money is not always an easy subject to talk about, but if you are working a budget with more than one person, communication is key! You can't effectively run a budget if both people are not on the same page. In the same way, if you have older kids making purchasing decisions, it's important that they become a part of the conversation, as well (within reason). Here are a few steps to making your communication more effective.

Agree on your budget – While this seems really basic, it's better done sooner than later. It is crucial that you agree on your budget with your spouse. Two people working towards a common goal can accomplish so much, but if someone isn't on board, then it's kind of like driving a car without four wheels--you probably won't go very far very fast. Maybe you're the "money person" in your family and you spent a lot of time working on the budget, figuring it all out and creating a plan. Don't forget to talk things over and make sure that the budget works for everyone involved and that everyone understands the goals and reasons behind the budget.

Make talking about money normal – I personally am not the "money person" in our family. I always managed my own money before I was married, but my husband is very detail oriented, so he prefers to be in charge of the budget. One of the things I appreciate about him is that he makes talking about money normal. It's a constant conversation in our home. We know exactly where we are, he gives me updates, and there isn't any stress involved. I know typically what I affectionately refer to as "money meetings" are sometimes heated conversations, but talking about your budget and letting each other know where you stand shouldn't have to be a big sit-down conversation all the time. It should be an ongoing conversation on a daily basis. For example, my husband might say to me, "We have almost spent all the money in the XYZ budget," and I can just say. "Okay, thanks for letting me know." It's about the communication.--if I'm not putting the receipts into the budget, then I don't always know where we stand, so I rely on him to keep me updated so that we can work together. Just because he enters the expenses into the budget doesn't mean that I'm not also responsible for the spending and keeping things in line.

Make your budget easy to access – I think this is the advantage to using the online envelope method for managing your budget. Multiple people can access the same budget at the same time. That means both users are seeing in real time the changes to each envelope. This is so helpful if you have two people working on daily expenses from a debit card or checking account. It allows you to make real time updates and both people to have access to all the information. I really think this is key to keeping your budget in control.

Keep your goals in mind – One thing that keeps me motivated when working our budget gets stressful is keeping our long-term and big goals in mind. My husband often gives me reports of where we stand in terms of reaching our big goals, and that's so encouraging to see progress, so if you start to feel yourself falling away from your budget, take a look at just how far you have come. Maybe it's how much debt you have paid off, how much you've saved, how much you were able to give, or other goals you're reaching by sticking to your budget. It's always good to go back to these goals and remind yourself why it's important to stay on track.

Day 20: Review Your Budget with Your Spouse

Now is a great time to talk over your budget with your spouse and family. If you haven't taken the time to talk through things, remember that it's also important to listen to and address any fears or concerns they have. Getting everyone on board and focusing on achieving goals together will help build unity in your family and within your budget.

Budgeting with Kids:

Kids are an important part of a successful budget. Don't forget to share your goals and dreams with your kids. It's easy for kids to hear "no we can't" or "we don't have the money" over and over again and not realize that the sacrifice is for a greater purpose later on. So help your kids dream with you. If you're saving for a

How to Make a Budget Work for You

vacation, remind them that you might not be able to eat out tonight because you can save that money for vacation, and maybe try planning a special dinner out during vacation that they can look forward to with you.

Day 21

Balance Your Income Before Spending

We have another great reminder today that when you get paid, it's important to take the time to focus on your budget and correctly appropriate your income before spending it.

How to Balance Your Income

If you are living paycheck to paycheck, it's easy to want to jump in the car and head to Wal-Mart with your debit card as soon as you get paid, However, it's really important to take some time to put your income into the correct categories and stay organized. The discipline of doing this will save you a lot of headaches and a lot of money.

One of the biggest tendencies that you want to avoid in a tight budget is the urge to be super tight with your money for a few weeks then run out and splurge as soon as you feel like you have money again. The problem with this spending habit is that you tend to lead yourself straight back into the cycle by overspending early in the pay period and then feeling strapped for cash late in the pay period. One of the biggest successes in your budget will be re-training yourself to have more disciplined spending habits.

How to Make a Budget Work for You

One of the best ways I know of to make sure you have enough money to last through the entire pay period (Especially if you get paid monthly) is to pay yourself an "allowance" on a weekly basis.

I'm all about keeping things simple, so I would highly recommend setting yourself a weekly "payday" for your cash accounts. If you take out lunch money, food, entertainment, gas, etc. on a weekly basis in cash, then you'll basically be giving yourself an allowance each week for your cash-based accounts. What happens is you might run out of lunch money on Wednesday and have to take your lunch on Thursday and Friday, but you'll have cash available again on Friday when your "pay yourself" day rolls around. The advantage to this method is that you don't end up feeling like you are depriving yourself for a long period of time; instead, it's more spread out and consistent and over time, so you'll be better controlled when it comes to spending.

Day 21: Setting up a Pay Yourself Deal

Take some time to figure out how much money you need to take out in cash or, if you are not planning on using cash, make yourself a list of how much money you can spend in each category on a weekly basis. This will help you pace out your spending. It's also a good idea to take time to pick a day when your budget will reset, using your payday or even the day after payday if you want to be able to get everything into your budget before the spending starts. I would recommend using the same day of the week you get paid on. If you get paid on the end of the month, maybe try using every Monday or every Friday to keep things consistent.

Balance Your Income Before Spending

Budgeting with Kids:

I'm a big proponent of teaching kids to work, so we give our kids jobs they can do around the house. I also like to teach them to wait since sometimes the best things in life aren't from instant gratification, so we have a "payday" at our house even for our kids. Every Sunday might we add up how many tasks they have completed and we pay them all at once. It also makes it easier to teach them to put the money in their budget categories when you're paying them once a week rather than giving them money all week long. I find that when we pay them all week long, we forget to be as disciplined about where the money ends up.

Day 22

Track & Carry Over Set-Back Accounts

Today we are going to talk about set-back accounts. These are the accounts you have in your budget that are saving for larger payments you make on an inconsistent basis, such as property taxes or, in some cases, auto insurance, saving for a car funds, and other items like this that you don't pay for on a monthly or a weekly basis.

How to Track & Carry Over Set Back Accounts

I use the term set-back accounts to define anything that you are saving for over multiple pay periods. So, if you're saving for a car or setting back a "car payment" to save to pay cash for a new car, these are set-back accounts--they aren't monthly or weekly spending accounts, but they are things you are planning and preparing for in your budget.

One of the most important things you want to remember about your budget is that you want to not only track your everyday spending purchases, but you also want to make sure that everything in your checking and savings accounts are "assigned" somewhere, even if that somewhere is to a savings category in your budget. What this allows you to do is know that if you're saving $100 a month towards auto insurance that you pay every six months, you know exactly how much you have

How to Make a Budget Work for You

in that budget category at any given time. When it's time to pay your auto insurance bill every six months, the money is already set aside and assigned to that task, so you're not scrambling at the last minute to pay your bills.

I also think it's important to keep your money in your checking or savings accounts assigned to specific budget categories because you can help avoid overspending this way. If everything in your checking account that you think of as extra you just call savings, then you're not being specific enough with your goals. You will also find yourself overspending in other areas because you feel like you can just "cover it with your savings"--well, that kind of defeats the purpose of savings, doesn't it :)

I like to track all of my budget categories the same way. I would highly recommend either using a spreadsheet or an online envelope management system to track your categories. That way, you can track all types of categories in one place. Your set-back categories will accumulate a balance over the weeks and months. Then, when you make a payment or purchase, you deduct that amount from your category.

It is also a good idea to go ahead and carry over the balance of your other budget categories rather than emptying out all your spending accounts at the end of the pay period. For example, we budget about $10-$20 more than we need on a weekly basis for gas, but sometimes the price fluctuates, and so does our driving, but instead of spending that money on something else or moving it at the end of the pay period, I leave it in the gas category, and then I have a cushion if the price goes up, or if we need to take a road trip, travel for sporting events, etc. Remember, you most likely based your budget categories on yearly or monthly expenses, so you may spend less some weeks and more the others; that's ok if you're carrying over your categories, because in the long run it will start to average out. The key is being disciplined enough not to take the money out when you have extra, because you might need that the next week or pay period and you don't want to continuously be taking from one category to cover others.

Budgeting with Kids:

In most cases, this same principle works with kids. We only take our kids shopping to spend their "spend" accounts about once a month so they learn to build up those categories and add to them every week even though we don't spend it that often. If you have older kids with jobs, they might have budgets like clothing, shoes, etc., where they would also want to assign a certain amount each paycheck, and then while they spend some, they might carry that leftover money in each category over until they need to make a bigger purchase. When it comes to kids, the principles are really very similar--it's just thinking through how you can simplify it for your child's age and understanding of money.

Day 23

Review & Maintain Your Budget Frequently

Now that you have a budget that you can work with on a daily basis, it's a good idea to maintain and manage your budget so that you don't end up having to start from scratch

How to Review & Adjust Your Budget

I can promise you just about one thing when it comes to your budget: no matter how much time you put into planning, tracking, and saving, you will almost always have to change your budget from your original. You will almost always have items you forgot to add that you need to include in your budget or items that you added and realized you didn't really need. Over time, adjusting your budget for the first three to six months and during any major life changes or pay increases will help you to maintain a more accurate budget and help to keep you from getting off track or having to start over.

Here are a few times in life when you should adjust and review your budget:

The initial three to six months of your budget – In order to get an accurate measure of what you're spending, it's important to review your budget at the beginning of each month. This is the time to add in things you were missing the month before and to adjust category amounts if you have some that are over-budgeted and others that are under budget.

Changes in Income – Another great time to review your budget is when you have a change in income. Extra money can be eaten up quickly if it's not budgeted and planned for, so make sure you adjust your budget when you get an increase or decrease in income.

Changes in lifestyle – Any time you have an addition to your family or a change in a family member's employment, get sick, move, or experience any other serious lifestyle change, it's important to evaluate how that will affect your budget. Even moving into a larger house or a newer house may affect your bills and expenses, so it's always a good idea to track these categories more closely when you have a major life change.

Loss of a job – A change from two incomes to one or a loss of employment completely are both great reasons to stop and do a massive evaluation of your budget. Even if you have an emergency fund, you want to make sure you adjust quickly to cover the loss of income so that you can make it as long as possible on your emergency fund. It's also a good idea to readjust again when you get a new job. Keeping your budget current with your actual income is critical to not overspending at any point in life. If you have an emergency fund for a job loss (say three to six months of expenses), then you need to incorporate "pay yourself" into your budget and try to be even more disciplined.

Review & Maintain Your Budget Frequently

Every time you adjust your budget, I recommend starting with items that have additional income then adding that additional income to other categories. That's the easiest way to balance. If you need to take money away from categories, you'll have to decide which categories are the least important

Budgeting with Kids:

Talk over changes in the budget with your kids. It's important that your family work together on a budget. They may need to know that these changes are just for a short time, or we need to be able to make a change in this category (say eating out less) so that we can afford to go on the vacation we are planning this summer. These discussions help kids to be on board with everything happening in the budget and also teaches valuable lessons about adjusting expenses according to income frequently so that you can avoid overspending.

Day 24

Create a Debt Reduction Plan

Documents You Will Need:

> **Debt Summary Worksheet**

One of the most common goals for creating a budget is to reduce, pay down, and eliminate debt. Today we are going to talk about how to create an action plan for reducing your debt using your budget.

How to Create a Debt Reduction Plan

When you were creating your budget, you should have included current debts in your list of expenses and budget categories. If you have a car payment, you most likely have a budget category for your car loan payment each month. The same should also be true for your other debts such as student loans, credit card balances, and outstanding medical bills. Each of these categories should at least have the minimum monthly payment to keep you current on your debts. So Step 1 is maintaining and not falling behind on these debts, and Step 2 is that we want to create an action plan for attacking and reducing the debt over time.

Start by listing your outstanding debts smallest to largest:

How to Make a Budget Work for You

One of the first steps to paying down and eliminating debt is to identify the debt. Create a debt list, with each item listed from smallest to largest by the full amount owed (not the monthly payment amount).

A plan for attacking debt:
At some point, if you want to reduce your debt you need to create a plan. Step 1 would be to stop accumulating new debt. You can't dig yourself out of a hole if you're still digging deeper, so cut up your credit cards and commit right now to stop adding to your debts. Hopefully, you've already worked through most of your expenses and adjusted your lifestyle to live within your means via the **Budget Planning Worksheet** I have provided, so the idea of overspending and having to charge an item or take out a loan should be something that's not a daily part of your life anymore. If you're still spending more on your credit card than you can pay off at the end of the month after making a budget, then you are more than likely overspending and you need to go back and re-evaluate your budget.

I have a three-step plan for attacking debt using your **Debt Summary Worksheet** that I mentioned above.

Step 1 – Pay the minimum monthly payment on all current debts.

Step 2 – Create a "debt reduction" category and put all the extra money in this category towards the first item on your list (the smallest balance).

Step 3 – When the first debt is paid off, the money that was going towards that item gets added to your Debt

Create a Debt Reduction Plan

Reduction category and you start attacking Item Number 2 on your list.

You can continue adding the money from the minimum monthly payments for each item you pay off to your Debt Reduction category, and you'll start to see this growing and your debt reduction power increasing! This is where you start to see traction. Eventually, when your debts are gone, you'll have all that money left over to add to your budget and savings! Eliminating debt is one of the first steps to building wealth!

Adding to your debt reduction fund:
One thing that's really important to remember is that if you are making your monthly payments and then spending everything else you make, you aren't actually reducing your debt--you are maintaining it. In order to reduce your debt, you may need to reduce some of your budget categories for a short time in order to add money to your debt reduction category.

Another idea for reducing debt is to have a garage sale or sell items that are no longer used or needed. You can quickly start to eliminate a few items off your list using this method, which will free up money in your budget to add to your debt reduction category.

And finally, you can start adding in jobs to increase your income. Even $50 a week can go a long way in paying down debt, so picking up a weekend job or a job for one or two nights a week short-term might be a great way to get a jump start on reducing your debt.

How to Make a Budget Work for You

Create a Debt Summary Sheet

Hopefully, you have already created your **Debt Summary Worksheet** in some of the first steps of creating your budget. If not, you can use this **Debt Summary Worksheet** to list all of your debts (small and large) in order from smallest to largest based on the outstanding balance. Note: we're not using the monthly payment amount or the interest rate this time--just the total overall balance. When you reduce one debt, you'll have more money to put towards the next item on your list, so it's faster to start paying items off if you work from smallest to largest.

Budgeting with Kids:

Kids often don't understand the concept of debt, but what they do understand is spending money on something you already have. Most of the time it's easy for kids to assume that we "paid" for something when we used our credit card. They don't understand that we are still responsible for that payment later on in life. Help your kids understand this concept by showing them what you owe and explaining that once you pay for these items, you'll have more money to spend on other things that you might be sacrificing right now. One idea is to create a Debt Countdown list, just listing the items you are paying off, and hang it on your fridge (you don't have to list the amounts, just the items in order). Then when you pay off a debt, let your kids help you cross that off the list. You could also use a set of paper chains with the names of each item written on the paper rings. Let them tear off the ring when the debt is paid down. This is a great way to create a visual reminder of the debts going away for little ones, and it encourages them to work towards the goals with you as a family

Day 25

Plan for Unexpected Expenses

Nothing will get your budget off track faster than having unexpected expenses come up. This could be anything from a car wreck, natural disasters, a loss of employment, or other life changes that you don't see coming. Planning for these expenses can be tricky because you don't know they are coming. By creating a general emergency fund, you can more effectively handle these situations in life.

How to Create an Emergency Fund

There are a few different levels to creating your emergency fund. I highly recommend starting with the first level of $1,000 then increasing your emergency fund as you move along in your savings plan. If you have a lot of debt, you will need to put more money into your debt reduction plan than your emergency fund. Once you have paid off your outstanding debt, you can work on increasing your emergency fund to the six-month level.

Basic emergency fund: $1,000 - Everyone, regardless of how much money you have, should strive to have a minimum of $1000 in your bank account as an emergency fund. You can cover a lot of unexpected expenses with $1,000, and having that money available

How to Make a Budget Work for You

will help you avoid having to reach for a credit card in time of need. Anytime you take from your emergency fund, that should become your number one priority--to repay up to the $1000 mark. Basically, what this allows you to do is borrow from yourself rather than borrowing from a credit card in times of need.

Short-term emergency fund: Three months of expenses – Each family's short-term emergency fund will be a different amount. You will need to take your family budget and determine what costs you would still incur if you lost your income. Then, take that monthly amount and multiply it times 3. That number is your short-term emergency fund. This will be your cushion if you lose your income and need to live off savings for a short period of time. This amount also will help you cover emergencies which require you to repair a car or the house or pay unexpected hospital bills.

Long-term emergency fund: Six months of expenses – If you have a lot of debt to pay off, it might be a while before you reach your long-term emergency fund goals. Your long-term emergency fund should be about twice the size of your short-term emergency fund. You may or may not decide that you want to have six months of expenses, but in today's job market it is something that I would highly recommend if you're in the financial position to accomplish this.

When to start your emergency fund –
Emergencies can happen any time--you never know if you'll be in a car wreck tomorrow, if your car will die and need a new transmission, or if your house will be hit by a hailstorm. Things happen--it's a part of life--so planning ahead for unexpected situations can save you so much time, stress, and money. If you don't have any

Plan for Unexpected Expenses

savings, or any emergency fund at all, I would start right now working towards this goal. You may even want to put your debt reduction plan on hold until you have $1000 in your emergency fund. This will help prevent you from going further into debt. Remember, in order to eliminate debt, you have to first stop the debt cycle, and having an emergency fund is step one in this process!

Once you have $1,000, I would recommend paying off your debts. You may decide you'd rather have a little more (say around $3,000) in your emergency fund just in case, but you have to remember that the money you aren't paying towards your debts is costing you interest each month! So it's a good idea to start attacking your outstanding debts as soon as you can. After paying off your debt, you can begin saving for your three months of living expenses then move on to the six month mark. Personally, we slowed down once we hit three months. At that point, we split the money going towards our emergency fund with retirement savings, so it took a little longer to go from three to six months, but we were also saving tax-free for retirement, so that was a personal decision on our part. It just goes to show that there isn't any right or wrong way to go about this-- everyone's personal situations and goals are different, so remember to look at your overall situation when making these decisions.

Determine your Emergency Fund Levels

Now is a great time to determine your three emergency fund levels. You should start with the $1,000 emergency fund, then add up your living expenses that you would need for a month and multiply that times three for your

How to Make a Budget Work for You

short-term emergency fund and times six for your long-term emergency fund. Write these three amounts on your budget somewhere, or maybe add them to your goals list that we created in the beginning. These are great financial goals that can be measured specifically. This will give you a resource to refer back to in the future when you start saving towards your larger emergency fund goals.

Budgeting with Kids:

As your kids get older, it's important to teach them to save for the unexpected. Remember to talk to your kids about the importance of an emergency fund. I know it's really easy to complain when you have to pay for a new appliance or car repairs, but try to focus on the positive. Small comments like, "I'm so glad we had been saving for our emergency fund so that we could pay for this car repair" will go a long way in teaching your kids the importance of saving, planning, and preparing.

Day 26

Plan for the Future

One of the most important things to remember when planning your budget is to remember to not only plan for your current expenses but to also plan for the future.

The Importance of Planning for the Future

One of the downfalls of a budget can often be that you spend every dollar you bring in. Even when you see your income increasing, it can be easy to start assigning extra income to categories that you enjoy rather than saving that money for the future.

Make the future a priority – One of the easiest ways to save for the future is by making your retirement savings a priority. If you work for a company that allows you to take 401k savings out of your check, this will force you to set aside your retirement savings before you begin spending.

Take advantage of benefits- Some companies offer a matching program for retirement savings. If you have the ability to put in the maximum amount that can be matched, then you can take advantage of the additional

How to Make a Budget Work for You

savings that aren't coming out of your own money. These types of benefits are to your advantage, so take the time to understand your companies pension and 401k matching programs.

Save consistently – If you don't have the ability or option to save with your company into a traditional 401k plan, then you will need to be more disciplined on your own. One of the most important factors of saving for retirement and the future is to save consistently. If you can set aside a small amount over a long period of time, the consistency and compounding of interest on your money can add up quickly.

Once you have $1000, I would recommend paying off your debts.

Evaluate Your Future Options

Take some time to do some research on your options for saving for the future. You may need to look into different retirement and IRA options, or check with your Human Resources Manager at work regarding the different options your company provides. Knowing your benefits and the details of each will help you make the wisest decisions for your own future.

Also, take some time to determine how much you can be saving for your retirement right now. It might not be much on a weekly or monthly basis, but every little bit adds up, and the earlier you start, the more you will have in your nest egg when you retire. By the time you finish paying off your debt, you should be saving around 10-15% of your income towards retirement goals, depending on your age and living standards. I would highly recommend that at some point you meet with a

Plan for the Future

financial planner to help you determine the best goals and methods for your own individual needs.

Budgeting with Kids:

Most kids don't understand the importance of saving for long-term and unknown goals. We are beginning to encourage our kids to save money in a savings account, which allows them to save long-term and reduces the desire to spend that money. By opening a savings account and letting kids add their Save money to the savings account, you are teaching these long-term disciplines, which will stick with them in life.

Day 27

Don't Forget to Give

I am so excited about today's topic because it is one that is near and dear to my heart. I love to give, and I love that saving money and budgeting has enabled me to give more, so today we are talking about the importance of adding giving into your budget.

The Importance of Giving

One of the things I love most about having a budget is not only planning and preparing for my family's future but being able and ready to give to those in need. If you haven't already, I would highly encourage you to set up a Giving category in your budget. This might be something that is a flexible account where you add money when you are blessed with a little extra, or something you make a priority, depending on where you are on your savings journey.

My husband and I have a Giving category; it's one of the first categories we add to each month, and by having this money set aside we are free to give without regret (knowing it isn't affecting our other savings and spending goals), and also it encourages us to look for ways to give and help with others' needs.

Every once in a while, when I am talking about budgeting, people look at me and ask if I feel like a budget is "restrictive." I guess I can see how people find a budget restrictive, but to me it's very freeing. I love knowing exactly what I am able to spend/give in each area, and I can make the best decisions for my family at each point in life. Let me explain this a little better. When it comes to giving, if I know that I have $50 a week, for example, in my Giving category, when I hear of a need, whether it's a church ministry, missionary, local family facing a challenge, or a food bank in need of supplies, I don't have to stress over whether I should give or not--and I don't have to move money around to make it happen. I can instantly meet needs that come into my life using this category, and it's a blessing to me to be able to give in this way because it's already planned for and budgeted for.

If we don't spend the money in our Giving account one week, we allow this to roll over and add up. In time, you may find larger needs that you can meet with a larger amount of money. You may also determine that you want to sponsor a child or a specific ministry on a monthly or annual basis. We do a little of both with our giving money, we have set programs that we give to as well as additional money that can be given where there is a need. To me it's a blessing to be able to use what God has given me to meet the needs of those that God places in my life. Something I should also point out is that our Giving category is separate from our Tithe category; we give 10% of all income back to our local church before any other budget categories are met, so the Giving category is what we are able to do above and beyond that.

Don't Forget to Give

Determining Your Giving Plan

Remember what is right for me and my family won't necessarily be right for you and your family. I really believe that giving allows you to not only bless others but to better put in perspective all that you have been given. Sometimes it's not until we reach beyond ourselves to meet the needs of others that we really begin to understand how blessed we are.

Take some time to set up a giving plan. You need to determine how much you want to put in your giving category and whether this will be something you add to out of each paycheck or if it will be a flexible account you add to when you receive additional income. Also, take some time to determine different causes and ministries that are important to you. Giving to something you believe in and to help people who are less fortunate than you will help you see the benefits of using your money to benefit others.

Budgeting with Kids:

Something that's important for us to remember as adults--but also for us to teach our kids--is that giving doesn't always require money. There are so many ways that we can give of our time and our talents without spending one dime. Look for ways that you and your kids can give back to the community. It might be donating old toys and clothes you no longer use or need to a shelter or serving an elderly couple in need. Taking meals to friends and family members who are in a time of need is also a great way to show others we love and care about them without having to give in a monetary way.

Day 28

Track Progress Towards Your Goals Monthly

Documents You Will Need:

- **Financial Goals Worksheet**

Do you remember back in the very beginning how we talked about **setting goals**? I really encouraged you to dream big and to write down your goals because it's important when you get into the daily process of working your budget.

The Importance of Tracking Progress Towards Goals

Nothing has helped us move towards our financial goals faster than writing these goals down and breaking them into smaller more attainable goals. If your goals include getting out of debt, it's a good idea to not only say, "I'm going to get out of debt," but also to list out each debt and start working on them one-by-one from smallest to largest. It's also motivating to start with the total amount of debt and to review how much you have paid off in total each month. For example, if you have $50,000 in debt, after you've paid off $20,000 or $30,000 of this, you start to see the light at the end of the tunnel because you can track your progress and see how far you have come.

How to Make a Budget Work for You

My husband and I love to review our financial goals frequently. By taking a look at where we stand in our savings goals, we are motivated to make wiser decisions on a daily basis because those financial goals are always in front of us. Right now, we are saving to pay cash for a house. When we look at how far we have come in the last five years and how close we are getting to accomplishing our goal, it motivates us to maybe turn down purchases that we might normally make (like new couches or a new TV) in order to put as much money as possible towards our goal.

By continually keeping our goals in front of us, we start to see all of our decisions both big and small in light of our dreams. When we put things in perspective like this on a monthly basis, we make smarter long-term decisions and avoid impulse purchases that can add up quickly in light of our larger long-term goals.

How to Track Your Progress

Now is a great time to pull out your **Financial Goals Worksheet.** Hopefully you have already listed your major goals and then broken this down into milestones. These smaller milestones are easier to accomplish. What I love to do is first look at Milestone 1 only. Work as hard as you can to accomplish this mini goal! That way when you achieve your goal, you can celebrate! I also love to put deadlines on these mini goals and work hard towards them, you may not accomplish every goal by your deadline date, but you will probably be further ahead than if you hadn't pushed yourself towards that deadline.

Track Progress Towards Your Goals Monthly

Everyone likes to feel like they are accomplishing something so don't focus on everything you want to do. The big picture can often feel very overwhelming. Instead, focus on the smaller, more attainable goal and what you have already accomplished. So if you have $50,000 in debt, you can either focus on the overwhelming number or focus on your success and how much you have paid off so far. I love looking at what I have accomplished because it makes me realize that I can accomplish my goals. Looking at the total number sometimes is overwhelming, but in small steps it's easier to see our dreams and goals realized.

Budgeting with Kids:

It is also important to teach our kids to track their progress and to keep their goals in mind. When my son is walking through the store and he says, "I want something," then I have him write this down on a Wish List (similar to a goals list, but this is a list of items he wants to use his Spend money on). About once a week, he likes to sit down and count his spend money. By counting the money and looking at his Wish List, he can see his progress towards his goals. It also motivates him to do items that he can get paid for over the next week because he wants to add to his Spend money and reach his goals.

Day 29

Share Your Successes With Others

Today is another one of my favorite topics. Not only is it important to track your progress towards your goals, but you should also make it a priority to share your successes (and dare I say failures) with those around you. Your story is just that--your story--and no matter how big or small the successes, it's important to share that with close friends and family and allow them to support you in your journey!

The Importance of Sharing Your Journey

Something that encouraged me in life a few years ago is the saying, "Regardless of where you are in life, there's always someone following behind you--find that person and teach them." I love this saying because we are all at different stages in our savings journey. You may be paying off debt, but you can encourage someone else to just get started. You may be saving for retirement, and you can encourage someone else to start planning for their future. Regardless of where you are in life, there is someone who you can teach from both your successes and your failures.

Now that you have developed your financial goals and started working towards them, take the time to share your goals with friends and family members in your life. You don't have to run around telling these to everyone you see, but take the time to share them with someone who you have a close relationship with. I want to encourage you to find at least two people. The first person should be someone you respect who can motivate and encourage you in your journey. The second should be someone you have influence with, someone who maybe you can motivate to take the first step. By having both aspects of accountability and encouragement, you will have partners to celebrate with along the way as you start to accomplish your financial goals.

Sharing Your Successes

You don't have to be really formal in sharing your goals. I don't really recommend a big sit down conversation, and I actually think it's better when you're sharing your goals in the midst of conversations about life, where you are, and what you're currently working on. It's really easy to let our goals slide when we don't have any accountability. Just telling someone you're working hard to try to pay off your debt is a great way to motivate yourself to stick to your plans. On the flip side, if you have someone who has walked in your same shoes before, they are a great person to talk with when the going gets tough, because sometimes sticking to your budget and paying down debt when everyone else around you seems to be buying everything you want can be tough. You need those cheerleaders in your life to motivate and encourage you during the tough times.

Now, once you've shared your goals, don't forget to go back to those same friends and family members and let them know when you accomplish your goals. I can still remember having coffee with one of my mentors and letting her know we were going to finally pay off our

Share Your Successes With Others

mortgage. She was so excited for us, and she was able to celebrate with us because this was something she herself had accomplished and something she knew we had been working on for years. Because I had shared our successes and failures with her along the way, she understood just how excited we were, and she was able to celebrate with us because she had been a part of the journey.

Budgeting with Kids:

Your kids are a great outlet for sharing your goals and your successes. Depending on the ages of your kids you can really have fun with this by celebrating different milestones along the way. If you have a really tight budget that doesn't allow for eating out, maybe you decide as a family that when you reach each milestone under one of your goals, you'll celebrate by going out to dinner. Or you may decide that if you accomplish a larger goal like paying off all your debt, that you'll save for a family vacation after that. Kids can also be a great accountability resource. I know my kids are great about reminding me of everything I said I would do or not do. If you don't plan to spend money on something, let your kids know--they will be sure to remind you in those situations where you might be tempted. :)

Day 30

Encourage Others

As you have started creating and maintaining your personal budget, I am hoping that you have gained a better understanding of your money and how to make smart decisions when it comes to your finances. Regardless of where you are on your journey, you have come a long way just by committing to your budget and taking the time to set it up and execute your personal plan. So many people fail in finances because they fail to plan. You are ahead of the curve simply because you have a plan and you are working towards it. Now it's time to look around and find someone who you can encourage to walk in the same path.

The Importance of Encouraging Others

I absolutely love seeing people encourage others. It doesn't matter how much debt you have paid off--or maybe you are actually working on a budget and you have your categories defined and working for the first time in your life. You can be an encouragement to someone following in your footsteps. Maybe it's a friend a family member or even your children. Taking time to look around you and encourage others is a great place to start!

You can encourage others in several ways, here are a few ideas to get you started:

How to Make a Budget Work for You

Share your personal journey - Everyone loves to hear about personal experiences. Even if your story is a little different, you can encourage others by sharing where you have come from. I will never forget the challenge of making our budget work when my son was first born and I had quit my job. I know that learning the strategies of couponing was a method for me to focus my energy and make things balance again. That motivation and that part of my story drives me each day as I post deals and tips for people who need and want to save money on not only groceries but everything they buy. I also remember the dedication it took to our budget to reach our goal of paying off our mortgage. We spend years working towards that goal, and while it wasn't always easy, the end result was so worth it! I can completely sympathize with someone living in tight circumstances in order to reach their goals, and I want to encourage people to accomplish more than they think they can. So take some time to share your story, your personal journey, no one can argue with that, and it can be a great source of encouragement for others in the same situation.

Share resources - Maybe you have a favorite book. Maybe it's a website or an ebook that really made things click for you. It's easy to recommend resources to friends, but it can also be a huge blessing if you just purchase the book with a sweet note, or allow a friend to borrow something that helped you along the way. Sharing resources can encourage those who are following in your footsteps.

Celebrate with others - I've already mentioned how important it is to celebrate your own milestones, but others need people to stand beside them in not only their failures but also their successes! Be willing to celebrate others' successes and try not to be jealous. We all have different situations and income levels, so it's not a competition-- remember that you can celebrate with friends and family members who are accomplishing their goals, and that's a great way to motivate and encourage them to continue towards even bigger goals.

Start at class or accountability group – You may or may not feel qualified to lead a class, but you can easily facilitate a program like Financial Peace by Dave Ramsey, or you can set up an accountability group. If you have several friends all working through financial issues, sometimes just a support group to keep going forward can be the encouragement that you and others in the group need.

Budgeting with Kids:

Kids are another great outlet for encouragement. All of our kids at some point in life need that encouragement to keep saving, to stay disciplined, and to stay focused. It's so easy for little ones and teenagers alike to get impatient in their savings or to get into patterns of spending that are unhealthy. As a parent, you are in the ideal situation to encourage and motivate your kids in the right direction. So take the time to talk with your kids about money and to motivate and encourage them in the right direction.

Day 31

Teach Your Children

I am sure that if you have been following this entire process, you have picked up on one thing: I am not only passionate not only about teaching other people about money, but I am a *huge* believer in teaching kids from an early age how to handle money.

The Importance of Teaching Your Children

One of the things I have become extremely aware of over the last few years is that not only do my decisions affect my husband and I, but our kids are immensely affected by all of my decisions--both good and bad. I want to pass on a legacy to my kids. I don't want them to just grow up thinking Mom was that "coupon lady" or she was super tight with her money and never bought anything. I want my kids to understand why we make the decisions we make and how they can make the same decisions.

Over the last few weeks, my son and I have had several great conversations about why we buy things, how we make those decisions, and how to make not just a good decision but the best decision. I want him to have his own money and make his own decisions--to learn the value of working hard and the pride that comes from working hard and saving for something you really want. I also want to teach my kids to give, that others might not have what they have but they can make a difference and make another child smile. These things might seem like small things in the grand scheme of life to others, but I believe they are vitally important in how my kids will handle their own money when they grow up.

Here are a few ideas of how you can teach your children to handle money:

Let them earn money - We have started our kids really little, teaching them that money doesn't grow on trees. It requires work, which isn't always easy, but it can be rewarding. Earlier this week, I offered my son the opportunity to earn $1 by cleaning the baseboards in our house. I didn't force him to do this; I let him make the decision because this was a job. He could either choose to do the work and get the reward or he could choose to play. He decided he would do the cleaning, and about halfway though he looked at me and said, "This is harder than I thought it would be." I just laughed because isn't that what we all think about life some days. It might just be $1, and my son might only be 5 right now, but he can still learn valuable lessons about earning money, and I can promise you that he will think twice about spending that dollar that he worked so hard for.

Encourage budgeting - Regardless of your kids' ages you can encourage them to budget their money. This looks different at different ages, but with little kids I love the three budget categories: Give, Save, Spend. As your kids get older, you might consider including clothing, lunch money, gas money, insurance, car savings, and other categories that are important to your kids.

Talk about money – Constantly and consistently make talking about money a part of your life. I am surprised how many parents don't talk with their kids about money. My kids know we don't buy something when we walk in the store that we didn't plan to buy. If we want something, we put it on a list for next time. We also only buy what we can afford, and we talk about making wise decisions--not just when they are making purchases but also when *we* are making purchases. Right now, we are saving to buy a new house. Our kids understand that we are saving our money and that sometimes we make decisions with this in mind. By including kids in the conversations about money and making it a normal part of life, we are teaching as we go by encouraging them in right methods and sharing the pitfalls of bad decisions we or others may have made with money so that they can learn from our mistakes.

Start at savings account – Kids often don't understand long-term savings. Especially if you have a spender by nature, they may want to spend everything they have rather than putting it away in a savings account. By starting a savings account and consistently taking your money to the bank, you are building healthy habits of savings. In the long run, as your kids get older they will begin to see the benefits of savings (I would suggest tracking your "Save" money about once a month, but it can be as frequently as you want).

Let them make mistakes – I know this seems very counter-intuitive, but sometimes letting kids make small mistakes now that teach valuable lessons in the long term can actually be better for them. For example, if they are saving for something that they really want,

How to Make a Budget Work for You

then they want to make an impulse purchase, you can gently remind them that might not be the smartest decision, but letting them make a mistake when it's something that doesn't really matter might be a great way to teach them great lessons.

I know sometimes we all need to learn from experience, and it's better for kids to make bad decisions when they are little and learn from them than to make big mistakes later on in life. Now, keep in mind I don't let my kids decide all the time what they are going to buy. I do believe in guiding them and teaching them, but there are always those times when you need to learn your own lessons. As a parent, you know your kids best, so it's just important to keep in mind that sometimes we learn the most through failure.

Every kid is different, and you know your kids best. I know that no one solution will work for everyone, but it's so important that you take the time to make teaching your kids about money a priority. It's a practical skill that will help them no matter where they end up in life.

Live With Passion

You did it! I wish I could be there to celebrate with you because I know you are on a path to changing your life forever! Over the years, there have been many seasons in life and also in our finances. I am not sure that one season is better than the other, but all have taught us important life lessons. I hope that you take your budget and let it adjust and grow with you. I want to be there to cheer you along! I'd love to hear about any success you have in paying down debt, living within your budget, and also giving all around the world! I know that these simple principles laid out within this book have transformed our lives. We went from two incomes to one, struggling to make ends meet and paying down debt, to living a debt-free life where we can give freely! It's a transformation that was hard work but has brought us so much joy!

As you walk through the next few months and years, go back to your budget frequently. If it doesn't work, if there's something that is hard to maintain or an area that's constantly giving you problems, adjust and work on it. I know that personally we have had seasons where

How to Make a Budget Work for You

we have gotten off track, and sometimes it's hard to get back on track, but every time we do I feel very satisfied about where we are and all that we can accomplish! Starting fresh is a great way to motivate yourself and get back into the lifestyle of savings.

Keep your goals in front of you. These are the visions that drive the daily decisions you are making. When you accomplish one goal, set a new one. It's not always about perfection--it's about progress! Keep moving forward and someday you'll look back and realize just how far you have come!

www.ingramcontent.com/pod-product-compliance
Lightning Source LLC
Chambersburg PA
CBHW071433180526
45170CB00001B/326